The Sponsor Couple Program for Christian Marriage Preparation

For Better and For Ever

Dialogue Packet

Robert Ruhnke, C.SS.R.

Liguori
ONE LIGUORI DRIVE
LIGUORI MO 63057-9999

Imprimi Potest:
William A. Nugent, C.SS.R.
Provincial, St. Louis Province
The Redemptorists

Imprimatur:
Monsignor Maurice F. Byrne
Vice Chancellor, Archdiocese of St. Louis

Scripture texts used in this work are taken from
the NEW AMERICAN BIBLE, copyright © 1986, by the
Confraternity of Christian Doctrine, Washington,
DC, and are used by permission of copyright
owner. All rights reserved.

Cover and internal design
by Pam Hummelsheim

SPECIAL THANKS

I am especially grateful to Monsignor Ed
Randall for coaxing me into family life
ministry.

There is a special place in my heart for
Sharon Barrett, Rob and Syl Degeyter,
Michelle Dumas, Gale and Mary Gaither,
John and Sharon Harry, Chuck and Carolyn
Lamar, Robert and Kathy Menotti, Lou and
Jacky Morgan, Bill and Rita Orth, Robert and
Pat Strobel, Jerry and Mary Velasquez, and
Jerry and Mary Jo Wilt, who have taught me
most of what I know about Christian marriage
and the building of relationships.

I am grateful to Father Carl Arico, Maureen
Bacchi, Charlie Balsam, Mary Boone, Karen
Camerino, Dr. Harry Croft and Benay Croft,
Sister Mary Dennison, Rabbi Edwin
Friedman, Kathy Grant, Harville Hendrix,
Wally and Winnie Honeywell, Marie Howard,
Michael and Joan Hoxsey, Sister Jane
Kammer, Father Sam Maranto, Reverend
Dick Murray, Paula Ripple, Charlie Schraub,
Reverend Diane Woolard, and Father Jim
Young, who have coaxed and challenged me
to look at life in new ways.

I remember fondly the late Roger
Marchand, managing editor of the books and
pamphlets department at Liguori Publications.
More than anyone else, he believed this
program should be published.

Finally, I thank Pauline Ruhnke, my
mother, who continues to teach me.

Contents

Evening One: Sharing About Our Families
Opening and Closing Prayers 5
Dialogue Session for Evening One 7-8, 11-12, 15-16, 19-20
Take-home Pages 9-10, 13-14, 17-18, 21-22

Evening Two: Further Sharing About Our Families
Opening and Closing Prayers 23
Dialogue Session for Evening Two 25-40

Evening Three: Effective Marital Communication
Opening and Closing Prayers 41
Dialogue Session for Evening Three 43-58

Evening Four: Marriage Is Intimate
Opening and Closing Prayers 59
Dialogue Session for Evening Four 61-75

Evening Five: A Covenant of Life and Love
Opening and Closing Prayers 77
Dialogue Session for Evening Five 79-93
Preparing the Marriage Ceremony 95

This Dialogue Packet contains:

One copy of the "Opening and Closing Prayer" (pages 5, 23, 41, 59, 77) for each evening. This page is shared by *both couples*, the sponsors and the engaged.

One copy of "Preparing the Marriage Ceremony" (page 95).

Four copies of all other pages: one for each person. In some activities there are different questions for the sponsor couple and the engaged couple.

EVENING 1

Sharing About Our Families

Opening Prayer

A reading from Matthew 18:19-20.

Again, I say to you, if two of you agree on earth about anything for which they are to pray, it shall be granted to them by my heavenly Father. For where two or three are gathered together in my name, there am I in the midst of them.

The sponsor couple reads aloud the following prayer:

Lord, the four of us gather this evening in your name. We are confident that you are here, in our midst.

As sponsor couple and engaged couple we know each other only slightly. Each of us is a little scared and wondering what our evening together will be like. We ask you, Lord, to fill us with your Spirit of wisdom and truth. Help us to relax and trust one another. Help us this evening to share with one another about the family in which we grew up. Amen.

Closing Prayer

The engaged couple reads aloud the following prayer:

We thank you, Lord, for giving each of us the wonderful treasure of human life. We have remembered and shared together a great deal about our families. We have remembered good times and hard times. We are most grateful for the people in our lives who have shown us how to love.

We thank you, Lord, for *always* loving each of us. In our courtship and marriage, you are helping us imitate your unending love. Amen.

1. The Floor Plan of Your Childhood Home

Using a separate sheet of paper, draw a picture of the floor plan of the home or apartment where you lived as a child, before age ten. Indicate details such as who shared which bedrooms and bathrooms and closet space, the location of the television set(s), and other details that had special significance for you. If you lived in several different homes or apartments, draw the one that you remember the best or the one that was the most significant for you.

2. Your Present Family Structure

Using a separate sheet of paper, make a diagram of your present family structure. (See example.)
Use lines to indicate relationships to spouses and children.
Use squares for *men* and circles for *women*.
Use × to indicate those who have *died*.
Use / / for a *divorce*.
Use ⌣ to indicate strong/close relationships.
Use ⌇ to indicate difficult relationships.

Sample Family

The following diagrams of John and Mary, an engaged couple, can be used as a model. In the diagram, note that:

1. John has a strong/close relationship with his mother, Peg.
2. John has two children by a previous marriage to Alice.
3. John has a difficult relationship with his sister, Sue.
4. John's parents, Peg and Tim, had no brothers or sisters.
5. All four of John's grandparents have died.
6. John is engaged to Mary.
7. Mary's mother died, and her father, Ted, married a second wife, Sally.
8. Mary has a difficult relationship with her father's second wife, Sally.
9. Mary has always been close to her sister, Joy.
10. Joy is married to Bob and has two children.
11. Mary's mother's parents are Jim and Nancy.
12. Ted's parents have died.

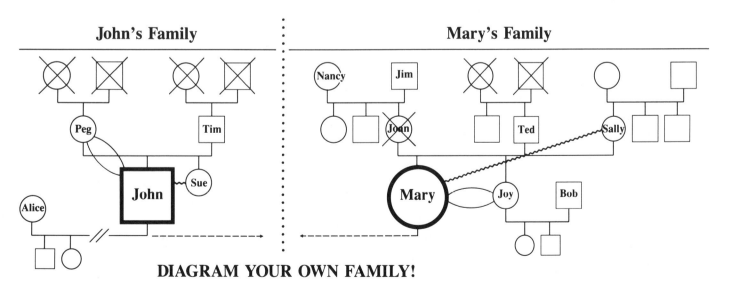

DIAGRAM YOUR OWN FAMILY!

Questions for Private Reflection and Dialogue

Take a few minutes by yourself to answer the questions and complete the statements. After you have done this, there will be time to compare answers and dialogue about your reflections.

Remember that there are no "right" or "wrong" answers. Simply express what you truthfully think and feel.

1. Who has been the most important member of my family? _____ Why? _____
_____

2. Who has been the key "parent" in my life? (This could be a natural parent or another adult.) _____
Why? _____
_____

3. My description of this relationship is _____
_____

4. Who has been the family member most likely to have problems? _____ What kind of problems? _____
_____

5. How has the death of family members affected the rest of the family? _____
_____

6. What has been the effect of divorce and/or remarriage on my family? _____
_____

7. To whom in the family do I feel closest? _____ Why? _____
_____

8. From whom in the family do I feel most distant? _____ Why? _____
_____

9. How have I related to each of my brothers and sisters? How did each of them treat me?
How did each of them relate to my parents? _____
_____

Name	My relationship to him/her	His/Her relationship to me	His/Her relationship to parents
_____	_____	_____	_____
_____	_____	_____	_____

10. The major strengths of my family are _____
_____

11. The major weaknesses of my family are _____
_____

12. I would describe my family as _____
_____

13. What I like most about my family is _____
_____

14. What I like least about my family is _____
_____

15. The one way I wish my family were different is _____
_____

16. (Circle one) I am *mostly happy* or *mostly unhappy* about my family. Why? _____
_____

Take-home Page: Family Patterns of Behavior

The following is a list of behavior patterns that are common in many families. On your own after this evening session, go through this list and indicate the patterns of behavior that happened in your own family. Also indicate whether you consider these to be healthy or unhealthy patterns of behavior.

O Often   **H** Healthy
S Sometimes   **U** Unhealthy
N Never   **N** Not sure

1. Pressure to make good grades .... [ ]   [ ]
2. Reward for making good grades .... [ ]   [ ]
3. Dominating father .... [ ]   [ ]
4. Dominating mother .... [ ]   [ ]
5. Frequent/serious illness .... [ ]   [ ]
6. Psychological depression .... [ ]   [ ]
7. Adequate/healthy sex education..................... [ ]   [ ]
8. Financial security................................. [ ]   [ ]
9. Seeking social status .... [ ]   [ ]
10. Parental unemployment .... [ ]   [ ]
11. Alcoholism .... [ ]   [ ]
12. Drug abuse .... [ ]   [ ]
13. Smoking .... [ ]   [ ]
14. Physical/sexual abuse............................. [ ]   [ ]
15. Divorce .... [ ]   [ ]
16. Harsh punishment................................ [ ]   [ ]
17. Frequent yelling .... [ ]   [ ]
18. Physical affection/emotional support................ [ ]   [ ]
19. Negligent/overly permissive parents................. [ ]   [ ]
20. Trusting parents .... [ ]   [ ]
21. Family prayer .... [ ]   [ ]
22. Sunday worship .... [ ]   [ ]
23. Joyful family gatherings........................... [ ]   [ ]
24. Political arguments............................... [ ]   [ ]
25. Being on time.................................... [ ]   [ ]
26. Being "the best" .... [ ]   [ ]

Other patterns not listed above:

27. _____ [ ]   [ ]

28. _____ [ ]   [ ]

29. _____ [ ]   [ ]

Take-home Page: Interviews With Family Members and Close Friends

Before the second evening, interview (a) one or both of your parents; (b) a brother and/or sister; (c) a close friend of your family of origin. You can interview as many people as you wish, but it is best to interview one person at a time.

The more people you interview, the more information you will gather. You will also see that different people are likely to have different memories of the *same* family experiences!

In arranging the interview, ask the person to spend twenty or thirty minutes with you. Explain that you would like to talk with them about your recollections of growing up, your relationship with them, and their place in your family. If they are hesitant to meet with you, assure them that this will be a pleasant and helpful interview and not something to fear.

Write the responses from each individual on a separate sheet of paper.

During the Interview:

1. Show your drawing of the floor plan of the place where you lived as a child. See if the other person has the same memories or can add any details.
2. Share your diagram of the family. See if the other person can add people or names you may have forgotten in your extended family. Ask the person about the details surrounding births and deaths and marriages and divorces. Ask them about particularly helpful or difficult relationships.
3. Share your chart of patterns of behavior. (You may choose just to talk about it and not reveal all the information on your chart.) Ask the other person what patterns of behavior he or she remembers.

After the Interviews:

Write your answers to these questions in the space provided.

1. What memories do people have about your family that are significantly different from your own? _____
   _____

2. What do these different recollections say to you about past events? _____
   _____

3. If any of your brothers or sisters have married, give key examples where your family's principal patterns of behavior are/are not being duplicated in the family of your brother or sister? _____
   _____

4. What have you learned/gained from these interviews with your own family members and persons who know your family? _____
   _____

After you have completed the interviews, and before the second session, share all of this in dialogue with your partner.

1. The Floor Plan of Your Childhood Home

Using a separate sheet of paper, draw a picture of the floor plan of the home or apartment where you lived as a child, before age ten. Indicate details such as who shared which bedrooms and bathrooms and closet space, the location of the television set(s), and other details that had special significance for you. If you lived in several different homes or apartments, draw the one that you remember the best or the one that was the most significant for you.

2. Your Present Family Structure

Using a separate sheet of paper, make a diagram of your present family structure. (See example.)

Use lines to indicate relationships to spouses and children.

Use squares for *men* and circles for *women*.

Use × to indicate those who have *died*.

Use / / for a *divorce*.

Use ⌣ to indicate strong/close relationships.

Use 〜〜 to indicate difficult relationships.

Sample Family

The following diagrams of John and Mary, an engaged couple, can be used as a model. In the diagram, note that:

1. John has a strong/close relationship with his mother, Peg.
2. John has two children by a previous marriage to Alice.
3. John has a difficult relationship with his sister, Sue.
4. John's parents, Peg and Tim, had no brothers or sisters.
5. All four of John's grandparents have died.
6. John is engaged to Mary.
7. Mary's mother died, and her father, Ted, married a second wife, Sally.
8. Mary has a difficult relationship with her father's second wife, Sally.
9. Mary has always been close to her sister, Joy.
10. Joy is married to Bob and has two children.
11. Mary's mother's parents are Jim and Nancy.
12. Ted's parents have died.

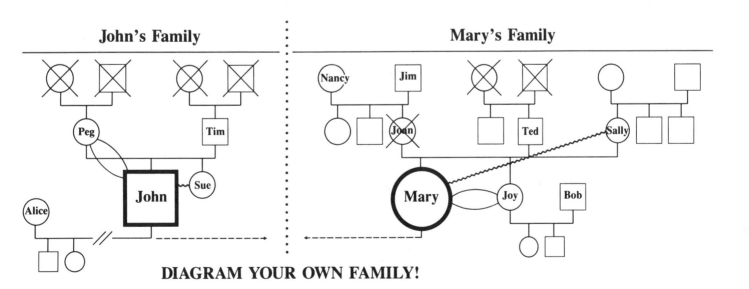

John's Family **Mary's Family**

DIAGRAM YOUR OWN FAMILY!

Questions for Private Reflection and Dialogue

Take a few minutes by yourself to answer the questions and complete the statements. After you have done this, there will be time to compare answers and dialogue about your reflections.

Remember that there are no "right" or "wrong" answers. Simply express what you truthfully think and feel.

1. Who has been the most important member of my family? _____ Why? _____
   _____

2. Who has been the key "parent" in my life? (This could be a natural parent or another adult.) _____
   Why? _____
   _____

3. My description of this relationship is _____
   _____

4. Who has been the family member most likely to have problems? _____ What kind of problems? _____
   _____

5. How has the death of family members affected the rest of the family? _____
   _____

6. What has been the effect of divorce and/or remarriage on my family? _____
   _____

7. To whom in the family do I feel closest? _____ Why? _____
   _____

8. From whom in the family do I feel most distant? _____ Why? _____
   _____

9. How have I related to each of my brothers and sisters? How did each of them treat me?
   How did each of them relate to my parents? _____

Name	My relationship to him/her	His/Her relationship to me	His/Her relationship to parents
_____	_____	_____	_____
_____	_____	_____	_____

10. The major strengths of my family are _____
    _____

11. The major weaknesses of my family are _____
    _____

12. I would describe my family as _____
    _____

13. What I like most about my family is _____
    _____

14. What I like least about my family is _____
    _____

15. The one way I wish my family were different is _____
    _____

16. (Circle one) I am *mostly happy* or *mostly unhappy* about my family. Why? _____
    _____

Take-home Page: Family Patterns of Behavior

The following is a list of behavior patterns that are common in many families. On your own after this evening session, go through this list and indicate the patterns of behavior that happened in your own family. Also indicate whether you consider these to be healthy or unhealthy patterns of behavior.

	O Often S Sometimes N Never	H Healthy U Unhealthy N Not sure
1. Pressure to make good grades	[ ]	[ ]
2. Reward for making good grades	[ ]	[ ]
3. Dominating father	[ ]	[ ]
4. Dominating mother	[ ]	[ ]
5. Frequent/serious illness	[ ]	[ ]
6. Psychological depression	[ ]	[ ]
7. Adequate/healthy sex education	[ ]	[ ]
8. Financial security	[ ]	[ ]
9. Seeking social status	[ ]	[ ]
10. Parental unemployment	[ ]	[ ]
11. Alcoholism	[ ]	[ ]
12. Drug abuse	[ ]	[ ]
13. Smoking	[ ]	[ ]
14. Physical/sexual abuse	[ ]	[ ]
15. Divorce	[ ]	[ ]
16. Harsh punishment	[ ]	[ ]
17. Frequent yelling	[ ]	[ ]
18. Physical affection/emotional support	[ ]	[ ]
19. Negligent/overly permissive parents	[ ]	[ ]
20. Trusting parents	[ ]	[ ]
21. Family prayer	[ ]	[ ]
22. Sunday worship	[ ]	[ ]
23. Joyful family gatherings	[ ]	[ ]
24. Political arguments	[ ]	[ ]
25. Being on time	[ ]	[ ]
26. Being "the best"	[ ]	[ ]

Other patterns not listed above:

27. _____	[ ]	[ ]
28. _____	[ ]	[ ]
29. _____	[ ]	[ ]

Take-home Page: Interviews With Family Members and Close Friends

Before you meet with your sponsor couple for the second evening, interview (a) one or both of your parents; (b) a brother and/or sister; (c) a close friend of your family. You can interview as many people as you wish, but it is best to interview one person at a time.

The more people you interview, the more information you will gather. You will also see that different people are likely to have different memories of the *same* family experiences!

In arranging the interview, ask the person to spend twenty or thirty minutes with you. Explain that you would like to talk with them about your recollections of growing up, your relationship with them, and their place in your family. Tell them that it will help you prepare for your marriage. If they are hesitant to meet with you, assure them that this will be a pleasant and helpful interview and not something to fear.

Write the responses from each individual on a separate sheet of paper.

During the Interview:

1. Show your drawing of the floor plan of the place where you lived as a child. See if the other person has the same memories or can add any details.
2. Share your diagram of the family. See if the other person can add people or names you may have forgotten in your extended family. Ask the person about the details surrounding births and deaths and marriages and divorces. Ask them about particularly helpful or difficult relationships.
3. Share your chart of patterns of behavior. (You may choose just to talk about it and not reveal all the information on your chart.) Ask the other person what patterns of behavior he or she remembers.

After the Interviews:

Write your answers to these questions in the space provided.

1. What memories do people have about your family that are significantly different from your own? _____

   _____

2. What do these different recollections say to you about past events? _____

   _____

3. If any of your brothers or sisters have married, give key examples where your family's principal patterns of behavior are/are not being duplicated in the family of your brother or sister? _____

   _____

4. What have you learned/gained from these interviews with your own family members and persons who know your family? _____

   _____

After you have completed the interviews, and before the second session, share all of this in dialogue with your partner.

1. The Floor Plan of Your Childhood Home

Using a separate sheet of paper, draw a picture of the floor plan of the home or apartment where you lived as a child, before age ten. Indicate details such as who shared which bedrooms and bathrooms and closet space, the location of the television set(s), and other details that had special significance for you. If you lived in several different homes or apartments, draw the one that you remember the best or the one that was the most significant for you.

2. Your Present Family Structure

Using a separate sheet of paper, make a diagram of your present family structure. (See example.)
Use lines to indicate relationships to spouses and children.
Use squares for *men* and circles for *women*.
Use ✕ to indicate those who have *died*.
Use / / for a *divorce*.
Use ⌣ to indicate strong/close relationships.
Use ∿∿∿ to indicate difficult relationships.

Sample Family

The following diagrams of John and Mary, an engaged couple, can be used as a model. In the diagram, note that:

1. John has a strong/close relationship with his mother, Peg.
2. John has two children by a previous marriage to Alice.
3. John has a difficult relationship with his sister, Sue.
4. John's parents, Peg and Tim, had no brothers or sisters.
5. All four of John's grandparents have died.
6. John is engaged to Mary.
7. Mary's mother died, and her father, Ted, married a second wife, Sally.
8. Mary has a difficult relationship with her father's second wife, Sally.
9. Mary has always been close to her sister, Joy.
10. Joy is married to Bob and has two children.
11. Mary's mother's parents are Jim and Nancy.
12. Ted's parents have died.

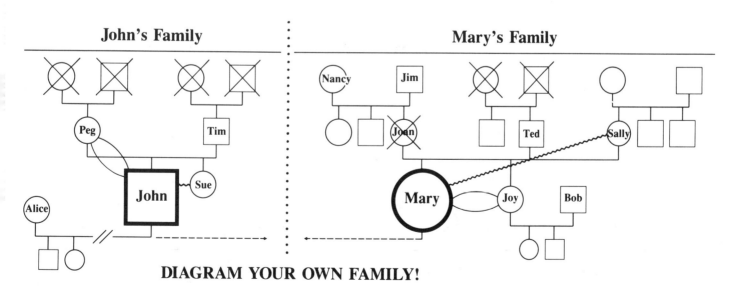

John's Family | **Mary's Family**

DIAGRAM YOUR OWN FAMILY!

Questions for Private Reflection and Dialogue

Take a few minutes by yourself to answer the questions and complete the statements. After you have done this, there will be time to compare answers and dialogue about your reflections.

Remember that there are no ''right'' or ''wrong'' answers. Simply express what you truthfully think and feel.

1. Who has been the most important member of my family? _____ Why? _____
   _____

2. Who has been the key ''parent'' in my life? (This could be a natural parent or another adult.) _____
   Why? _____
   _____

3. My description of this relationship is _____
   _____

4. Who has been the family member most likely to have problems? _____ What kind of problems? _____
   _____

5. How has the death of family members affected the rest of the family? _____
   _____

6. What has been the effect of divorce and/or remarriage on my family? _____
   _____

7. To whom in the family do I feel closest? _____ Why? _____
   _____

8. From whom in the family do I feel most distant? _____ Why? _____
   _____

9. How have I related to each of my brothers and sisters? How did each of them treat me?
   How did each of them relate to my parents? _____
   _____

Name	My relationship to him/her	His/Her relationship to me	His/Her relationship to parents
_____	_____	_____	_____
_____	_____	_____	_____

10. The major strengths of my family are _____
    _____

11. The major weaknesses of my family are _____
    _____

12. I would describe my family as _____
    _____

13. What I like most about my family is _____
    _____

14. What I like least about my family is _____
    _____

15. The one way I wish my family were different is _____
    _____

16. (Circle one) I am *mostly happy* or *mostly unhappy* about my family. Why? _____
    _____

Take-home Page: Family Patterns of Behavior

The following is a list of behavior patterns that are common in many families. On your own after this evening session, go through this list and indicate the patterns of behavior that happened in your own family when you were growing up. Also indicate whether you consider these to be healthy or unhealthy patterns of behavior.

O Often   **H** Healthy
S Sometimes **U** Unhealthy
N Never   **N** Not sure

1. Pressure to make good grades	[ ]	[ ]
2. Reward for making good grades	[ ]	[ ]
3. Dominating father	[ ]	[ ]
4. Dominating mother	[ ]	[ ]
5. Frequent/serious illness	[ ]	[ ]
6. Psychological depression	[ ]	[ ]
7. Adequate/healthy sex education	[ ]	[ ]
8. Financial security	[ ]	[ ]
9. Seeking social status	[ ]	[ ]
10. Parental unemployment	[ ]	[ ]
11. Alcoholism	[ ]	[ ]
12. Drug abuse	[ ]	[ ]
13. Smoking	[ ]	[ ]
14. Physical/sexual abuse	[ ]	[ ]
15. Divorce	[ ]	[ ]
16. Harsh punishment	[ ]	[ ]
17. Frequent yelling	[ ]	[ ]
18. Physical affection/emotional support	[ ]	[ ]
19. Negligent/overly permissive parents	[ ]	[ ]
20. Trusting parents	[ ]	[ ]
21. Family prayer	[ ]	[ ]
22. Sunday worship	[ ]	[ ]
23. Joyful family gatherings	[ ]	[ ]
24. Political arguments	[ ]	[ ]
25. Being on time	[ ]	[ ]
26. Being "the best"	[ ]	[ ]

Other patterns not listed above:

27. _____	[ ]	[ ]
28. _____	[ ]	[ ]
29. _____	[ ]	[ ]

Take-home Page: Interviews With Family Members and Close Friends

Before the second evening, interview (a) one or both of your parents; (b) a brother and/or sister; (c) a close friend of your family of origin. You can interview as many people as you wish, but it is best to interview one person at a time.

The more people you interview, the more information you will gather. You will also see that different people are likely to have different memories of the *same* family experiences!

In arranging the interview, ask the person to spend twenty or thirty minutes with you. Explain that you would like to talk with them about your recollections of growing up, your relationship with them, and their place in your family. If they are hesitant to meet with you, assure them that this will be a pleasant and helpful interview and not something to fear.

Write the responses from each individual on a separate sheet of paper.

During the Interview:

1. Show your drawing of the floor plan of the place where you lived as a child. See if the other person has the same memories or can add any details.
2. Share your diagram of the family. See if the other person can add people or names you may have forgotten in your extended family. Ask the person about the details surrounding births and deaths and marriages and divorces. Ask them about particularly helpful or difficult relationships.
3. Share your chart of patterns of behavior. (You may choose just to talk about it and not reveal all the information on your chart.) Ask the other person what patterns of behavior he or she remembers.

After the Interviews:

Write your answers to these questions in the space provided.

1. What memories do people have about your family that are significantly different from your own? _____
   _____

2. What do these different recollections say to you about past events? _____
   _____

3. If any of your brothers or sisters have married, give key examples where your family's principal patterns of behavior are/are not being duplicated in the family of your brother or sister? _____
   _____

4. What have you learned/gained from these interviews with your own family members and persons who know your family? _____
   _____

After you have completed the interviews, and before the second session, share all of this in dialogue with your spouse.

1. The Floor Plan of Your Childhood Home

Using a separate sheet of paper, draw a picture of the floor plan of the home or apartment where you lived as a child, before age ten. Indicate details such as who shared which bedrooms and bathrooms and closet space, the location of the television set(s), and other details that had special significance for you. If you lived in several different homes or apartments, draw the one that you remember the best or the one that was the most significant for you.

2. Your Present Family Structure

Using a separate sheet of paper, make a diagram of your present family structure. (See example.)
Use lines to indicate relationships to spouses and children.
Use squares for *men* and circles for *women*.
Use × to indicate those who have *died*.
Use / / for a *divorce*.
Use ⌣ to indicate strong/close relationships.
Use ∿ to indicate difficult relationships.

Sample Family

The following diagrams of John and Mary, an engaged couple, can be used as a model. In the diagram, note that:

1. John has a strong/close relationship with his mother, Peg.
2. John has two children by a previous marriage to Alice.
3. John has a difficult relationship with his sister, Sue.
4. John's parents, Peg and Tim, had no brothers or sisters.
5. All four of John's grandparents have died.

6. John is engaged to Mary.
7. Mary's mother died, and her father, Ted, married a second wife, Sally.
8. Mary has a difficult relationship with her father's second wife, Sally.
9. Mary has always been close to her sister, Joy.
10. Joy is married to Bob and has two children.
11. Mary's mother's parents are Jim and Nancy.
12. Ted's parents have died.

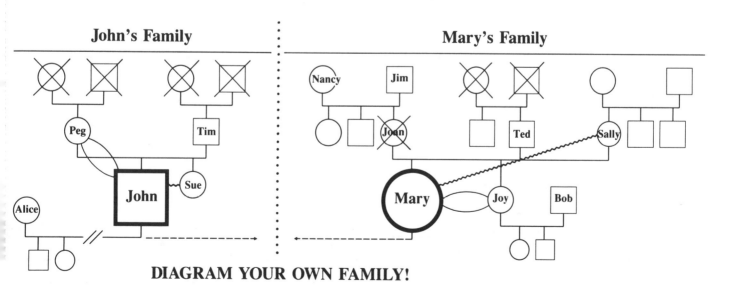

John's Family   Mary's Family

DIAGRAM YOUR OWN FAMILY!

Questions for Private Reflection and Dialogue

Take a few minutes by yourself to answer the questions and complete the statements. After you have done this, there will be time to compare answers and dialogue about your reflections.

Remember that there are no "right" or "wrong" answers. Simply express what you truthfully think and feel.

1. Who has been the most important member of my family? _____ Why? _____
   _____

2. Who has been the key "parent" in my life? (This could be a natural parent or another adult.) _____
   Why? _____
   _____

3. My description of this relationship is _____
   _____

4. Who has been the family member most likely to have problems? _____ What kind of problems? _____
   _____

5. How has the death of family members affected the rest of the family? _____
   _____

6. What has been the effect of divorce and/or remarriage on my family? _____
   _____

7. To whom in the family do I feel closest? _____ Why? _____
   _____

8. From whom in the family do I feel most distant? _____ Why? _____
   _____

9. How have I related to each of my brothers and sisters? How did each of them treat me?
   How did each of them relate to my parents? _____
   _____

Name	My relationship to him/her	His/Her relationship to me	His/Her relationship to parents
_____	_____	_____	_____
_____	_____	_____	_____

10. The major strengths of my family are _____
    _____

11. The major weaknesses of my family are _____
    _____

12. I would describe my family as _____
    _____

13. What I like most about my family is _____
    _____

14. What I like least about my family is _____
    _____

15. The one way I wish my family were different is _____
    _____

16. (Circle one) I am *mostly happy* or *mostly unhappy* about my family. Why? _____
    _____

Take-home Page: Family Patterns of Behavior

The following is a list of behavior patterns that are common in many families. On your own after this evening session, go through this list and indicate the patterns of behavior that happened in your own family when you were growing up. Also indicate whether you consider these to be healthy or unhealthy patterns of behavior.

	O Often S Sometimes N Never	H Healthy U Unhealthy N Not sure
1. Pressure to make good grades	[ ]	[ ]
2. Reward for making good grades	[ ]	[ ]
3. Dominating father	[ ]	[ ]
4. Dominating mother	[ ]	[ ]
5. Frequent/serious illness	[ ]	[ ]
6. Psychological depression	[ ]	[ ]
7. Adequate/healthy sex education	[ ]	[ ]
8. Financial security	[ ]	[ ]
9. Seeking social status	[ ]	[ ]
10. Parental unemployment	[ ]	[ ]
11. Alcoholism	[ ]	[ ]
12. Drug abuse	[ ]	[ ]
13. Smoking	[ ]	[ ]
14. Physical/sexual abuse	[ ]	[ ]
15. Divorce	[ ]	[ ]
16. Harsh punishment	[ ]	[ ]
17. Frequent yelling	[ ]	[ ]
18. Physical affection/emotional support	[ ]	[ ]
19. Negligent/overly permissive parents	[ ]	[ ]
20. Trusting parents	[ ]	[ ]
21. Family prayer	[ ]	[ ]
22. Sunday worship	[ ]	[ ]
23. Joyful family gatherings	[ ]	[ ]
24. Political arguments	[ ]	[ ]
25. Being on time	[ ]	[ ]
26. Being "the best"	[ ]	[ ]

Other patterns not listed above:

27. _____	[ ]	[ ]
28. _____	[ ]	[ ]
29. _____	[ ]	[ ]

Take-home Page: Interviews With Family Members and Close Friends

Before the second evening, interview (a) one or both of your parents; (b) a brother and/or sister; (c) a close friend of your family of origin. You can interview as many people as you wish, but it is best to interview one person at a time.

The more people you interview, the more information you will gather. You will also see that different people are likely to have different memories of the *same* family experiences!

In arranging the interview, ask the person to spend twenty or thirty minutes with you. Explain that you would like to talk with them about your recollections of growing up, your relationship with them, and their place in your family. If they are hesitant to meet with you, assure them that this will be a pleasant and helpful interview and not something to fear.

Write the responses from each individual on a separate sheet of paper.

During the Interview:

1. Show your drawing of the floor plan of the place where you lived as a child. See if the other person has the same memories or can add any details.
2. Share your diagram of the family. See if the other person can add people or names you may have forgotten in your extended family. Ask the person about the details surrounding births and deaths and marriages and divorces. Ask them about particularly helpful or difficult relationships.
3. Share your chart of patterns of behavior. (You may choose just to talk about it and not reveal all the information on your chart.) Ask the other person what patterns of behavior he or she remembers.

After the Interviews:

Write your answers to these questions in the space provided.

1. What memories do people have about your family that are significantly different from your own? _____
   _____

2. What do these different recollections say to you about past events? _____
   _____

3. If any of your brothers or sisters have married, give key examples where your family's principal patterns of behavior are/are not being duplicated in the family of your brother or sister? _____
   _____

4. What have you learned/gained from these interviews with your own family members and persons who know your family? _____
   _____

After you have completed the interviews, and before the second session, share all of this in dialogue with your spouse.

EVENING **2**

Further Sharing About Our Families

Opening Prayer

A reading from Matthew 1:1-2.

> The book of the genealogy of Jesus Christ, the son of David, the son of Abraham. Abraham became the father of Isaac, Isaac the father of Jacob, Jacob the father of Judah and his brothers.

The sponsor couple reads aloud the following prayer:

> Lord, in the genealogy of Jesus we can find both saints and sinners; people who were ever faithful, like Ruth; people who were guilty of terrible crimes, like David. Our own families are filled with both saints and sinners. We pray for all of them — living and dead — as we begin our sharing this evening. Amen.

Closing Prayer

The engaged couple reads aloud the following prayer:

> Dearest Lord God, we are your children. We are destined to live forever in your kingdom.
> We are also children of our individual families. We have been given what our families had to offer. We have inherited strengths and hopes and dreams and visions. We have also inherited weaknesses, prejudices, and fears.
> We place our trust in you. We believe that you are our Redeemer and Savior. We believe that our decision to enter into Christian marriage will set us on a path of salvation and healing and growth. With you as our guide and with the help of your grace, we will search together for ways to continue changing and growing so that we will be ever better lovers.
> Help us, Lord God, to learn how to use both our strengths and our weaknesses in the building of our marriage. Give us the wisdom to know that what may, at times, seem impossible to us, can be done if we allow you to help us. Amen.

Questions for Private Reflection and Dialogue

Take a few minutes by yourself to answer the questions and complete the statements. After you have done this, there will be time to compare answers and dialogue about your reflections.

Remember that there are no "right" or "wrong" answers. Simply express what you truthfully think and feel.

About Myself

1. In what ways do I see myself as a "product" of my family? _____

2. In what ways do I see myself as "different" from my family? _____

3. What sort of personality do I have? (Check one or more.)

   A. [ ] Leader
   B. [ ] Peacemaker
   C. [ ] Thinker
   D. [ ] Status Seeker
   E. [ ] Helper

   F. [ ] Clown
   G. [ ] Hard Worker
   H. [ ] Responsible One
   I. [ ] Artist
   J. [ ] Life of the Party

   K. [ ] Lover
   L. [ ] Expert at Many Things
   M. [ ] Victim
   N. [ ] (Other) _____

4. What does my personality type mean to me? _____

5. Why did I develop this kind of personality within my family? _____

6. My major strengths are _____

7. Which strengths have I "inherited" and which have I developed by myself? _____

8. How do I see these strengths affecting my relationships with people in my family, where I work, and with my friends? _____

9. My major weaknesses are _____

10. Which weaknesses have I "inherited" and which are a result of my own actions and lifestyle? _____

11. How do I see these weaknesses affecting my relationships with people in my family, where I work, and with my friends? _____

12. At the present time I would describe my personality as _____

ENGAGED PACKET

About My Partner

13. In what ways do I see my partner as a ''product'' of his or her family?_____
_____

14. In what ways do I see my partner as ''different'' from his or her family? _____
_____

15. What sort of personality do I see in my partner? (Check one or more.)

A. [ ] Leader	**F.** [ ] Clown	**K.** [ ] Lover
B. [ ] Peacemaker	**G.** [ ] Hard Worker	**L.** [ ] Expert at Many Things
C. [ ] Thinker	**H.** [ ] Responsible One	**M.** [ ] Victim
D. [ ] Status Seeker	**I.** [ ] Artist	**N.** [ ] (Other) _____
E. [ ] Helper	**J.** [ ] Life of the Party	

16. This personality type fits my partner because _____
_____

17. My partner developed this kind of personality within his or her family because _____
_____

18. My partner's major strengths are _____
_____

19. Which strengths are ''inherited'' and which has he or she developed independently? _____
_____

20. How do I see these strengths affecting his or her relationships with people in his or her family,
where he or she works, and with his or her friends?_____
_____

21. My partner's major weaknesses are _____
_____

22. Which weaknesses are ''inherited'' and which ones result from his or her own actions
and lifestyle?_____
_____

23. How do I see these weaknesses affecting his or her relationships with people in his or her family,
where he or she works, and with his or her friends?_____
_____

24. At the present time I would describe my partner's personality as _____
_____

The Power of Expectations and Assumptions

(Directions: After completing the "Questions for Private Reflection and Dialogue" for this evening, the engaged couple and the sponsor couple should read the information on this page. Then they should answer the questions on the pages after the reading, noting that there are different questions for the engaged couple and the sponsor couple.)

The choice of our marriage partner may seem mysterious even to people who know us well. "I don't know what she sees in him!" "Why is he so attracted to her?"

For ourselves, however, the choice is clear and strong. While we may find it difficult to give clear and logical reasons, we know we are making a good decision. Something within us tells us that our chosen one is the most likely person to fulfill our special hopes and dreams.

It is also very typical, usually not long after the honeymoon, for even the most committed spouses to wonder if they made a terrible mistake!

Why? Why is it that engaged couples who are deeply committed to "being different" and "making their marriage special" and "living happily ever after" turn into married couples who are pretty much like most other married couples?

A key to understanding and dealing with this phenomenon is to know about our *assumptions* and *expectations*.

Assumptions and expectations are the conscious (sometimes) or unconscious (more often) ideas we have about the world around us and the way we can best relate to other people. We inherit many of our assumptions from our family of origin. Our prejudices can be found here, as well as our highest ideals and goals. To a large degree our family has taught us the importance of saving money or spending money; the wisdom of smoking or not smoking; the correct way to do dishes and deal with illness. From our family we learn that there are right places to live, right kinds of friends to have, and right kinds of vacations to take! There are "correct" choices about politics and religion, the use of drugs and alcohol, and the place of religion in the family. Each of us has a perfectly correct theory or opinion about each of these ideas.

In fact, we know we are so right about all of these assumptions and expectations that we "take for granted" that all wise, intelligent, and reasonable people agree with us. Only fools would disagree. Of course, we believe that the people we can count on most to agree with us are those we love.

This tendency we each have to presume that others see things our way is called *projection*. Projection means that we expect another person — in this case, our partner — to have similar assumptions about life and relationships. Projection can be a real stumbling block to a successful marriage because we can frequently find ourselves at odds with many of our spouse's words and actions. We see their ideas and actions to be different from our own assumptions and expectations, and we begin to assume that there is something wrong with our spouse. Meanwhile, our spouse is also finding out that we think and act differently than he or she expected!

A good way to overcome the dead end of assumptions and projections is to take the time and effort to figure out *what* they are and *where* they came from. When we do this we can usually discover that we have a lot of *different* assumptions and expectations; and we can also trace them back to events and patterns of behavior in our family of origin.

The questions on the back of this page are meant to identify some of our assumptions and expectations about things we often tend to "take for granted." By bringing these assumptions and expectations to light, we can talk about how we developed these assumptions and expectations. Then we can decide what might be a good way to do things in our own marriage. We are free to keep our present assumptions and expectations, or we are free to make changes within ourselves to ways of thinking and talking and action that might be even better!

The important thing to know is that we have a choice!

Questions About Expectations and Assumptions

The questions on this page are for the engaged couple. The sponsor couple has slightly different questions. After each person has answered the questions on his or her page, the four people should share their responses.

1. I think I should be able to spend _____ dollars without consulting my spouse after we marry.
2. Of the two of us, _____ will be responsible for handling our family finances and making sure that bills are paid.
3. If my future spouse gets a job change that requires us to move to a different city or state, I will _____
_____
4. When do I think our first child will be born? (Guess the date of birth.) _____
5. With whose parents do I think we will spend the most time? _____
6. How and where will we celebrate Christmas or other special events? _____
_____
7. Which of us is more affectionate? _____ Which of us is more likely to make the first move in being affectionate? _____
8. My assumption about weekend worship is that we will _____
_____
9. Among the people I know, who has the best marriage? _____ What is the reason for their success? _____
_____

10. How will we manage the following chores?
    (H = Husband; W = Wife; B = Both)
    A. [ ] set the alarm for getting up
    B. [ ] fix breakfast
    C. [ ] get the newspaper
    D. [ ] make the bed
    E. [ ] plan supper
    F. [ ] do the dishes
    G. [ ] clean the house
    H. [ ] do the laundry
    I. [ ] shop for food

    J. [ ] open bills
    K. [ ] apologize to friends we hurt
    L. [ ] oversee repairs
    M. [ ] put gas and oil in car
    N. [ ] plan weekends
    O. [ ] decide on social events
    P. [ ] schedule weekend worship
    Q. [ ] pick up my dirty clothes
    R. [ ] write Christmas cards

11. The assumptions and expectations of mine that are different from those of my future spouse are _____
_____

Questions for Private Reflection and Dialogue

Take a few minutes by yourself to answer the questions and complete the statements. After you have done this, there will be time to compare answers and dialogue about your reflections.

Remember that there are no ''right'' or ''wrong'' answers. Simply express what you truthfully think and feel.

About Myself

1. In what ways do I see myself as a ''product'' of my family? _____

2. In what ways do I see myself as ''different'' from my family? _____

3. What sort of personality do I have? (Check one or more.)
   - A. [ ] Leader
   - B. [ ] Peacemaker
   - C. [ ] Thinker
   - D. [ ] Status Seeker
   - E. [ ] Helper
   - F. [ ] Clown
   - G. [ ] Hard Worker
   - H. [ ] Responsible One
   - I. [ ] Artist
   - J. [ ] Life of the Party
   - K. [ ] Lover
   - L. [ ] Expert at Many Things
   - M. [ ] Victim
   - N. [ ] (Other) _____

4. What does my personality type mean to me? _____

5. Why did I develop this kind of personality within my family? _____

6. My major strengths are _____

7. Which strengths have I ''inherited'' and which have I developed by myself? _____

8. How do I see these strengths affecting my relationships with people in my family, where I work, and with my friends? _____

9. My major weaknesses are _____

10. Which weaknesses have I ''inherited'' and which are a result of my own actions and lifestyle? _____

11. How do I see these weaknesses affecting my relationships with people in my family, where I work, and with my friends? _____

12. At the present time I would describe my personality as _____

About My Partner

13. In what ways do I see my partner as a ''product'' of his or her family?_____

_____

14. In what ways do I see my partner as ''different'' from his or her family? _____

_____

15. What sort of personality do I see in my partner? (Check one or more.)

A. [ ] Leader	**F.** [ ] Clown	**K.** [ ] Lover
B. [ ] Peacemaker	**G.** [ ] Hard Worker	**L.** [ ] Expert at Many Things
C. [ ] Thinker	**H.** [ ] Responsible One	**M.** [ ] Victim
D. [ ] Status Seeker	**I.** [ ] Artist	**N.** [ ] (Other) _____
E. [ ] Helper	**J.** [ ] Life of the Party	

16. This personality type fits my partner because _____

_____

17. My partner developed this kind of personality within his or her family because _____

_____

18. My partner's major strengths are _____

_____

19. Which strengths are ''inherited'' and which has he or she developed independently? ____

_____

20. How do I see these strengths affecting his or her relationships with people in his or her family, where he or she works, and with his or her friends?_____

_____

21. My partner's major weaknesses are _____

_____

22. Which weaknesses are ''inherited'' and which ones result from his or her own actions and lifestyle?_____

_____

23. How do I see these weaknesses affecting his or her relationships with people in his or her family, where he or she works, and with his or her friends?_____

_____

24. At the present time I would describe my partner's personality as _____

_____

The Power of Expectations and Assumptions

(Directions: After completing the "Questions for Private Reflection and Dialogue" for this evening, the engaged couple and the sponsor couple should read the information on this page. Then they should answer the questions on the pages after the reading, noting that there are different questions for the engaged couple and the sponsor couple.)

The choice of our marriage partner may seem mysterious even to people who know us well. "I don't know what she sees in him!" "Why is he so attracted to her?"

For ourselves, however, the choice is clear and strong. While we may find it difficult to give clear and logical reasons, we know we are making a good decision. Something within us tells us that our chosen one is the most likely person to fulfill our special hopes and dreams.

It is also very typical, usually not long after the honeymoon, for even the most committed spouses to wonder if they made a terrible mistake!

Why? Why is it that engaged couples who are deeply committed to "being different" and "making their marriage special" and "living happily ever after" turn into married couples who are pretty much like most other married couples?

A key to understanding and dealing with this phenomenon is to know about our *assumptions* and *expectations*.

Assumptions and expectations are the conscious (sometimes) or unconscious (more often) ideas we have about the world around us and the way we can best relate to other people. We inherit many of our assumptions from our family of origin. Our prejudices can be found here, as well as our highest ideals and goals. To a large degree our family has taught us the importance of saving money or spending money; the wisdom of smoking or not smoking; the correct way to do dishes and deal with illness. From our family we learn that there are right places to live, right kinds of friends to have, and right kinds of vacations to take! There are "correct" choices about politics and religion, the use of drugs and alcohol, and the place of religion in the family. Each of us has a perfectly correct theory or opinion about each of these ideas.

In fact, we know we are so right about all of these assumptions and expectations that we "take for granted" that all wise, intelligent, and reasonable people agree with us. Only fools would disagree. Of course, we believe that the people we can count on most to agree with us are those we love.

This tendency we each have to presume that others see things our way is called *projection*. Projection

means that we expect another person — in this case, our partner — to have similar assumptions about life and relationships. Projection can be a real stumbling block to a successful marriage because we can frequently find ourselves at odds with many of our spouse's words and actions. We see their ideas and actions to be different from our own assumptions and expectations, and we begin to assume that there is something wrong with our spouse. Meanwhile, our spouse is also finding out that we think and act differently than he or she expected!

A good way to overcome the dead end of assumptions and projections is to take the time and effort to figure out *what* they are and *where* they came from. When we do this we can usually discover that we have a lot of *different* assumptions and expectations; and we can also trace them back to events and patterns of behavior in our family of origin.

The questions on the back of this page are meant to identify some of our assumptions and expectations about things we often tend to "take for granted." By bringing these assumptions and expectations to light, we can talk about how we developed these assumptions and expectations. Then we can decide what might be a good way to do things in our own marriage. We are free to keep our present assumptions and expectations, or we are free to make changes within ourselves to ways of thinking and talking and action that might be even better!

The important thing to know is that we have a choice!

Questions About Expectations and Assumptions

The questions on this page are for the engaged couple. The sponsor couple has slightly different questions. After each person has answered the questions on his or her page, the four people should share their responses.

1. I think I should be able to spend _____ dollars without consulting my spouse after we marry.
2. Of the two of us, _____ will be responsible for handling our family finances and making sure that bills are paid.
3. If my future spouse gets a job change that requires us to move to a different city or state, I will _____
   _____
4. When do I think our first child will be born? (Guess the date of birth.) _____
5. With whose parents do I think we will spend the most time? _____
6. How and where will we celebrate Christmas or other special events? _____
   _____
7. Which of us is more affectionate? _____ Which of us is more likely to make the first move in being affectionate? _____
8. My assumption about weekend worship is that we will _____
   _____
9. Among the people I know, who has the best marriage? _____ What is the reason for their success? _____
   _____
10. How will we manage the following chores?
    (H = Husband; W = Wife; B = Both)

    A. [ ] set the alarm for getting up
    B. [ ] fix breakfast
    C. [ ] get the newspaper
    D. [ ] make the bed
    E. [ ] plan supper
    F. [ ] do the dishes
    G. [ ] clean the house
    H. [ ] do the laundry
    I. [ ] shop for food

    J. [ ] open bills
    K. [ ] apologize to friends we hurt
    L. [ ] oversee repairs
    M. [ ] put gas and oil in car
    N. [ ] plan weekends
    O. [ ] decide on social events
    P. [ ] schedule weekend worship
    Q. [ ] pick up my dirty clothes
    R. [ ] write Christmas cards

11. The assumptions and expectations of mine that are different from those of my future spouse are _____
    _____

Questions for Private Reflection and Dialogue

Take a few minutes by yourself to answer the questions and complete the statements. After you have done this, there will be time to compare answers and dialogue about your reflections.

Remember that there are no "right" or "wrong" answers. Simply express what you truthfully think and feel.

About Myself

1. In what ways do I see myself as a "product" of my family? _____
_____

2. In what ways do I see myself as "different" from my family? _____
_____

3. What sort of personality do I have? (Check one or more.)

   A. [ ] Leader   F. [ ] Clown   K. [ ] Lover
   B. [ ] Peacemaker   G. [ ] Hard Worker   L. [ ] Expert at Many Things
   C. [ ] Thinker   H. [ ] Responsible One   M. [ ] Victim
   D. [ ] Status Seeker   I. [ ] Artist   N. [ ] (Other) _____
   E. [ ] Helper   J. [ ] Life of the Party

4. What does my personality type mean to me? _____
_____

5. Why did I develop this kind of personality within my family? _____
_____

6. My major strengths are _____
_____

7. Which strengths have I "inherited" and which have I developed by myself? _____
_____

8. How do I see these strengths affecting my relationships with people in my family, where I work, and with my friends?_____
_____

9. My major weaknesses are _____
_____

10. Which weaknesses have I "inherited" and which are a result of my own actions and lifestyle? _____
_____

11. How do I see these weaknesses affecting my relationships with people in my family, where I work, and with my friends? _____
_____

12. At the present time I would describe my personality as _____
_____

About My Partner

13. In what ways do I see my partner as a "product" of his or her family?_____

_____

14. In what ways do I see my partner as "different" from his or her family? _____

_____

15. What sort of personality do I see in my partner? (Check one or more.)

A. [ ] Leader	**F.** [ ] Clown	**K.** [ ] Lover
B. [ ] Peacemaker	**G.** [ ] Hard Worker	**L.** [ ] Expert at Many Things
C. [ ] Thinker	**H.** [ ] Responsible One	**M.** [ ] Victim
D. [ ] Status Seeker	**I.** [ ] Artist	**N.** [ ] (Other) _____
E. [ ] Helper	**J.** [ ] Life of the Party	

16. This personality type fits my partner because _____

_____

17. My partner developed this kind of personality within his or her family because _____

_____

18. My partner's major strengths are _____

_____

19. Which strengths are "inherited" and which has he or she developed independently? _____

_____

20. How do I see these strengths affecting his or her relationships with people in his or her family,
where he or she works, and with his or her friends?_____

_____

21. My partner's major weaknesses are _____

_____

22. Which weaknesses are "inherited" and which ones result from his or her own actions
and lifestyle?_____

_____

23. How do I see these weaknesses affecting his or her relationships with people in his or her family,
where he or she works, and with his or her friends?_____

_____

24. At the present time I would describe my partner's personality as _____

_____

The Power of Expectations and Assumptions

(Directions: After completing the "Questions for Private Reflection and Dialogue" for this evening, the engaged couple and the sponsor couple should read the information on this page. Then they should answer the questions on the pages after the reading, noting that there are different questions for the engaged couple and the sponsor couple.)

The choice of our marriage partner may seem mysterious even to people who know us well. "I don't know what she sees in him!" "Why is he so attracted to her?"

For ourselves, however, the choice is clear and strong. While we may find it difficult to give clear and logical reasons, we know we are making a good decision. Something within us tells us that our chosen one is the most likely person to fulfill our special hopes and dreams.

It is also very typical, usually not long after the honeymoon, for even the most committed spouses to wonder if they made a terrible mistake!

Why? Why is it that engaged couples who are deeply committed to "being different" and "making their marriage special" and "living happily ever after" turn into married couples who are pretty much like most other married couples?

A key to understanding and dealing with this phenomenon is to know about our *assumptions* and *expectations*.

Assumptions and expectations are the conscious (sometimes) or unconscious (more often) ideas we have about the world around us and the way we can best relate to other people. We inherit many of our assumptions from our family of origin. Our prejudices can be found here, as well as our highest ideals and goals. To a large degree our family has taught us the importance of saving money or spending money; the wisdom of smoking or not smoking; the correct way to do dishes and deal with illness. From our family we learn that there are right places to live, right kinds of friends to have, and right kinds of vacations to take! There are "correct" choices about politics and religion, the use of drugs and alcohol, and the place of religion in the family. Each of us has a perfectly correct theory or opinion about each of these ideas.

In fact, we know we are so right about all of these assumptions and expectations that we "take for granted" that all wise, intelligent, and reasonable people agree with us. Only fools would disagree. Of course, we believe that the people we can count on most to agree with us are those we love.

This tendency we each have to presume that others see things our way is called *projection*. Projection means that we expect another person — in this case, our partner — to have similar assumptions about life and relationships. Projection can be a real stumbling block to a successful marriage because we can frequently find ourselves at odds with many of our spouse's words and actions. We see their ideas and actions to be different from our own assumptions and expectations, and we begin to assume that there is something wrong with our spouse. Meanwhile, our spouse is also finding out that we think and act differently than he or she expected!

A good way to overcome the dead end of assumptions and projections is to take the time and effort to figure out *what* they are and *where* they came from. When we do this we can usually discover that we have a lot of *different* assumptions and expectations; and we can also trace them back to events and patterns of behavior in our family of origin.

The questions on the back of this page are meant to identify some of our assumptions and expectations about things we often tend to "take for granted." By bringing these assumptions and expectations to light, we can talk about how we developed these assumptions and expectations. Then we can decide what might be a good way to do things in our own marriage. We are free to keep our present assumptions and expectations, or we are free to make changes within ourselves to ways of thinking and talking and action that might be even better!

The important thing to know is that we have a choice!

Questions About Expectations and Assumptions

The questions on this page are for the sponsor couple. The engaged couple has slightly different questions. After each person has answered the questions on his or her page, the four people should share their responses.

1. I think I should be able to spend _____ dollars without consulting my spouse.
2. Of the two of us, _____ is responsible for handling our family finances and making sure bills are paid. I (circle one) prefer to retain / would like to change this arrangement because _____

3. If my spouse gets a job change that requires us to move to a different city or state, I will _____

4. When do I think our next child will be born? (Guess the date of birth.) _____

5. With whose parents do we spend the most time? _____ How do I feel about this pattern of behavior? _____

6. How and where do we now celebrate Christmas and other special events? _____

   Why do I want to keep or change this pattern of behavior? _____

7. Which of us is more affectionate? _____ Which of us is more likely to make the first move in being affectionate? _____

8. My assumption about weekend worship is that we _____

9. Among the people I know, who has the best marriage? _____ What is the reason for their success? _____

10. How do we now manage the following chores?
    (H = Husband; W = Wife; B = Both)

    A. [ ] set the alarm for getting up   J. [ ] open bills
    B. [ ] fix breakfast   K. [ ] apologize to friends we hurt
    C. [ ] get the newspaper   L. [ ] oversee repairs
    D. [ ] make the bed   M. [ ] put gas and oil in car
    E. [ ] plan supper   N. [ ] plan weekends
    F. [ ] do the dishes   O. [ ] decide on social events
    G. [ ] clean the house   P. [ ] schedule weekend worship
    H. [ ] do the laundry   Q. [ ] pick up my dirty clothes
    I. [ ] shop for food   R. [ ] write Christmas cards

    What changes, if any, would I like to make? _____

11. The assumptions and expectations of mine that are different from those of my spouse are _____

Questions for Private Reflection and Dialogue

Take a few minutes by yourself to answer the questions and complete the statements. After you have done this, there will be time to compare answers and dialogue about your reflections.

Remember that there are no "right" or "wrong" answers. Simply express what you truthfully think and feel.

About Myself

1. In what ways do I see myself as a "product" of my family? _____

2. In what ways do I see myself as "different" from my family? _____

3. What sort of personality do I have? (Check one or more.)

   A. [ ] Leader   F. [ ] Clown   K. [ ] Lover
   B. [ ] Peacemaker   G. [ ] Hard Worker   L. [ ] Expert at Many Things
   C. [ ] Thinker   H. [ ] Responsible One   M. [ ] Victim
   D. [ ] Status Seeker   I. [ ] Artist   N. [ ] (Other) _____
   E. [ ] Helper   J. [ ] Life of the Party

4. What does my personality type mean to me? _____

5. Why did I develop this kind of personality within my family? _____

6. My major strengths are _____

7. Which strengths have I "inherited" and which have I developed by myself? _____

8. How do I see these strengths affecting my relationships with people in my family, where I work, and with my friends? _____

9. My major weaknesses are _____

10. Which weaknesses have I "inherited" and which are a result of my own actions and lifestyle? _____

11. How do I see these weaknesses affecting my relationships with people in my family, where I work, and with my friends? _____

12. At the present time I would describe my personality as _____

About My Partner

13. In what ways do I see my partner as a "product" of his or her family?_____
_____

14. In what ways do I see my partner as "different" from his or her family? _____
_____

15. What sort of personality do I see in my partner? (Check one or more.)

A. [ ] Leader   F. [ ] Clown   K. [ ] Lover
B. [ ] Peacemaker   G. [ ] Hard Worker   L. [ ] Expert at Many Things
C. [ ] Thinker   H. [ ] Responsible One   M. [ ] Victim
D. [ ] Status Seeker   I. [ ] Artist   N. [ ] (Other) _____
E. [ ] Helper   J. [ ] Life of the Party

16. This personality type fits my partner because _____
_____

17. My partner developed this kind of personality within his or her family because _____
_____

18. My partner's major strengths are _____
_____

19. Which strengths are "inherited" and which has he or she developed independently? _____
_____

20. How do I see these strengths affecting his or her relationships with people in his or her family,
where he or she works, and with his or her friends?_____
_____

21. My partner's major weaknesses are _____
_____

22. Which weaknesses are "inherited" and which ones result from his or her own actions
and lifestyle?_____
_____

23. How do I see these weaknesses affecting his or her relationships with people in his or her family,
where he or she works, and with his or her friends?_____
_____

24. At the present time I would describe my partner's personality as _____
_____

The Power of Expectations and Assumptions

(Directions: After completing the "Questions for Private Reflection and Dialogue" for this evening, the engaged couple and the sponsor couple should read the information on this page. Then they should answer the questions on the pages after the reading, noting that there are different questions for the engaged couple and the sponsor couple.)

The choice of our marriage partner may seem mysterious even to people who know us well. "I don't know what she sees in him!" "Why is he so attracted to her?"

For ourselves, however, the choice is clear and strong. While we may find it difficult to give clear and logical reasons, we know we are making a good decision. Something within us tells us that our chosen one is the most likely person to fulfill our special hopes and dreams.

It is also very typical, usually not long after the honeymoon, for even the most committed spouses to wonder if they made a terrible mistake!

Why? Why is it that engaged couples who are deeply committed to "being different" and "making their marriage special" and "living happily ever after" turn into married couples who are pretty much like most other married couples?

A key to understanding and dealing with this phenomenon is to know about our *assumptions* and *expectations*.

Assumptions and expectations are the conscious (sometimes) or unconscious (more often) ideas we have about the world around us and the way we can best relate to other people. We inherit many of our assumptions from our family of origin. Our prejudices can be found here, as well as our highest ideals and goals. To a large degree our family has taught us the importance of saving money or spending money; the wisdom of smoking or not smoking; the correct way to do dishes and deal with illness. From our family we learn that there are right places to live, right kinds of friends to have, and right kinds of vacations to take! There are "correct" choices about politics and religion, the use of drugs and alcohol, and the place of religion in the family. Each of us has a perfectly correct theory or opinion about each of these ideas.

In fact, we know we are so right about all of these assumptions and expectations that we "take for granted" that all wise, intelligent, and reasonable people agree with us. Only fools would disagree. Of course, we believe that the people we can count on most to agree with us are those we love.

This tendency we each have to presume that others see things our way is called *projection*. Projection means that we expect another person — in this case, our partner — to have similar assumptions about life and relationships. Projection can be a real stumbling block to a successful marriage because we can frequently find ourselves at odds with many of our spouse's words and actions. We see their ideas and actions to be different from our own assumptions and expectations, and we begin to assume that there is something wrong with our spouse. Meanwhile, our spouse is also finding out that we think and act differently than he or she expected!

A good way to overcome the dead end of assumptions and projections is to take the time and effort to figure out *what* they are and *where* they came from. When we do this we can usually discover that we have a lot of *different* assumptions and expectations; and we can also trace them back to events and patterns of behavior in our family of origin.

The questions on the back of this page are meant to identify some of our assumptions and expectations about things we often tend to "take for granted." By bringing these assumptions and expectations to light, we can talk about how we developed these assumptions and expectations. Then we can decide what might be a good way to do things in our own marriage. We are free to keep our present assumptions and expectations, or we are free to make changes within ourselves to ways of thinking and talking and action that might be even better!

The important thing to know is that we have a choice!

Questions About Expectations and Assumptions

The questions on this page are for the sponsor couple. The engaged couple has slightly different questions. After each person has answered the questions on his or her page, the four people should share their responses.

1. I think I should be able to spend _____ dollars without consulting my spouse.

2. Of the two of us, _____ is responsible for handling our family finances and making sure bills are paid. I (circle one) prefer to retain / would like to change this arrangement because _____

_____

3. If my spouse gets a job change that requires us to move to a different city or state, I will _____

_____

4. When do I think our next child will be born? (Guess the date of birth.) _____

5. With whose parents do we spend the most time? _____ How do I feel about this pattern of behavior? _____

_____

6. How and where do we now celebrate Christmas and other special events? _____

_____

Why do I want to keep or change this pattern of behavior? _____

_____

7. Which of us is more affectionate? _____ Which of us is more likely to make the first move in being affectionate? _____

8. My assumption about weekend worship is that we _____

_____

9. Among the people I know, who has the best marriage? _____ What is the reason for their success? _____

_____

10. How do we now manage the following chores?
    (H = Husband; W = Wife; B = Both)

    A. [ ] set the alarm for getting up   J. [ ] open bills
    B. [ ] fix breakfast   K. [ ] apologize to friends we hurt
    C. [ ] get the newspaper   L. [ ] oversee repairs
    D. [ ] make the bed   M. [ ] put gas and oil in car
    E. [ ] plan supper   N. [ ] plan weekends
    F. [ ] do the dishes   O. [ ] decide on social events
    G. [ ] clean the house   P. [ ] schedule weekend worship
    H. [ ] do the laundry   Q. [ ] pick up my dirty clothes
    I. [ ] shop for food   R. [ ] write Christmas cards

    What changes, if any, would I like to make? _____

11. The assumptions and expectations of mine that are different from those of my spouse are _____

_____

EVENING 3

Effective Marital Communication

Opening Prayer

A reading from the Letter to the Colossians 3:12-17.

Put on, then, as God's chosen ones, holy and beloved, heartfelt compassion, kindness, humility, gentleness, and patience, bearing with one another and forgiving one another, if one has a grievance against another; as the Lord has forgiven you, so must you also do. And over all these put on love, that is, the bond of perfection. And let the peace of Christ control your hearts, the peace into which you were also called in one body. And be thankful. Let the word of Christ dwell in you richly, as in all wisdom you teach and admonish one another, singing psalms, hymns, and spiritual songs with gratitude in your hearts to God. And whatever you do, in word or in deed, do everything in the name of the Lord Jesus, giving thanks to God the Father through him.

The sponsor couple reads aloud the following prayer:

Lord God, we give you thanks for our times of growth together. Send your Spirit over each of us so that day by day we may lay our hearts open to one another. May our love for each other grow ever stronger and more visible so that all who meet us will know of our love. Help us to love so completely that we are a sign to others of your own unconditional love for your people. We ask this in Jesus' name. Amen.

Closing Prayer

The engaged couple reads aloud the following prayer:

Lord God, we know that our love for one another is a blessing from you that can encourage us toward ever deeper love for you, as well as for one another.

The more we come to know one another, the better we appreciate how much we can offer one another in the way of understanding, appreciation, and support. We also know that each of us has areas of hurt and needs that can be touched and healed only with the power of your love.

Help us, Lord, to continue risking openness to one another. With you to help us overcome our fears, we can grow to be mature individuals and a strong couple who have much to offer the world around us. Amen.

The Value of Effective Communication

(Directions: The engaged couple and the sponsor couple should read the information on this page. They should discuss any ideas that need clarification before answering the questions that follow.)

When two people are truly "in love," they open the boundaries of their personal identities and let another person into the most intimate areas of their private selves. People in love can become so united that they think the same thoughts, like the same foods, and desire always to be together. When one person cries, the other tastes the salt of the tears!

For two people in love, the experience of togetherness can become much more important than one's personal identity. This deep union does have its advantages. It can feel cozy, protective, and secure. But it also has its limitations and can inhibit personal growth and individual choice. If lovers are going to continue growing as persons, it is necessary to be separate individuals as well as close companions.

A couple can achieve the proper balance between closeness and separateness in a relationship by developing effective communication methods. This does not come naturally, however, and what they have learned in the past may not be correct. Ideas about marital communication often come from the experiences of communicating with members of one's family of origin (parents, grandparents, brothers and sisters). This can present a problem since so many families and so many married couples have rather poor patterns of communication. Families of origin teach things like, "It is best not to talk about problems because it only makes them worse." They imply that "women have feelings and are emotional, but real men are those who do not let their emotions show." Family members come to believe that there are all sorts of things that are simply "not talked about." They also foster the myth that "if you really love me, you know what I want without me having to tell you."

Poor communication is a major factor in marital problems. Effective communication, on the other hand, can promote personal growth and maturity as well as mutual harmony. Every couple can learn to communicate more effectively. In improving one's communication skills, the first step is often the hardest. It involves admitting that there is a lot more to learn about each other than what is known from being "in love." The second step calls for recognizing that many of the communication patterns learned during one's growing up years may *not* be helpful patterns of behavior. The third step calls for couples to learn and practice some new skills.

The four major skills needed for effective marital communication are:

1. sharing my own inner thoughts and feelings;
2. hearing what the other has to share;
3. accepting myself and my spouse;
4. speaking my mind and heart with love.

This evening's questions and experiences are designed to help you learn and practice these four skills.

Questions for Private Reflection and Dialogue: Learning to Share and Hear About Our Differences

Skill #1 — Sharing. In writing your responses to these questions, try to share your inner thoughts and feelings as honestly as you can. Focus on your own personal experience by using "I messages" as much as possible (rather than writing about "you"). There is a special value in sharing your feelings rather than merely your opinions or theories.

Skill #2 — Listening. When you share what you have written, try to really listen to what the other person is saying. Resist the urge to react to or argue about what the other person is sharing. The best response is: "Tell me more about what you are feeling so that I can understand you more clearly."

1. How is my personality different from my partner's? _____

_____

2. The personality trait of my partner that I most admire is _____. The personality trait of my partner that I find difficult to tolerate and difficult to talk about is _____

3. In what ways are we an example of "opposites attract" and how do I feel about this? _____

_____

4. Recall a recent disagreement. Did it have anything to do with different assumptions or expectations, and how did we resolve it? _____

_____

5. What is a potential disagreement that is *likely* to happen in the future? _____

_____

6. My ideas about God, church, or religion are somewhat different from my partner's because I believe that _____

_____

7. What disagreements will arise over religion and how do I intend to deal with them? _____

_____

8. I admit that I do too much (smoking, working, playing, drinking alcohol, TV watching, complaining, arguing, pouting, spending time with friends, and so forth) _____

_____

My partner's excessive behaviors include _____

_____

I intend to deal with this by _____

_____

9. Toward my future in-laws, I feel _____

_____

My partner responds to this by _____

_____

10. Other than my partner, who is the person I confide in the most? _____ What does my partner think about my confiding in this person? _____

_____

11. Can I imagine sharing things with that person which I might not share with my partner? _____

How will this affect my relationship with my partner? _____

_____

12. The way we handled disagreements/problems in my family while I was growing up was
(Check the ones that best fit your family.)
   A. [ ] Avoidance. Problems were simply not talked about.
   B. [ ] Physical/verbal violence. Destructive fighting.
   C. [ ] Passivity. We ignored and denied our problems.
   D. [ ] Giving in. The most powerful always "won."
   E. [ ] Pouting. A way of warning others to stay away.
   F. [ ] Yelling and screaming. A way of punishing others.
   G. [ ] Withdrawal. Hiding from problems and disagreement.
   H. [ ] Manipulation. Covering conflict with gifts or promises.
   I. [ ] Compromise. We learned to give and take.
   J. [ ] Collaboration. We worked together for what was best.

13. At the present time, how are my partner and I dealing with differences and conflicts?
(Check the ones that are appropriate.)
   A. [ ] Avoidance. Problems are simply not talked about.
   B. [ ] Physical/verbal violence. Destructive fighting.
   C. [ ] Passivity. We ignore and deny our problems.
   D. [ ] Giving in. The most powerful "wins."
   E. [ ] Pouting. A way of warning others to stay away.

F. [ ] Yelling and screaming. A way of punishing others.

G. [ ] Withdrawal. Hiding from problems and conflict.

H. [ ] Manipulation. We cover conflict with gifts or promises.

I. [ ] Compromise. We have learned to give and take.

J. [ ] Collaboration. We work together for what is best.

14. Why am I comfortable/not comfortable (circle one) with our present method(s) of dealing with disagreements? _____

_____

15. I want my partner and I to deal with disagreements by _____

_____

16. Some guidelines that would help us be more successful in conflict resolution include _____

_____

Skill #3 — The Special Skill and Gift of Mutual Acceptance

(Directions: The engaged couple and the sponsor couple should read the information below. They should discuss any ideas that need clarification before answering the questions that follow.)

The third major skill of effective marital communication involves accepting the uniqueness of one another. In the language of marital communication, accepting goes beyond the standard dictionary definition of the word. The dictionary says that accepting means ''to receive willingly'' or ''to agree with'' or ''to give approval.'' Sometimes it is easy to ''accept'' in this way what your partner has to share about himself or herself. It is not as easy to accept thoughts and feelings and actions that you disagree with.

The accepting in this case calls for a decision to treasure and value the person (my spouse or myself) and resist the urge to reject or condemn the person as bad or evil because of what he or she is thinking or feeling or hoping or fearing or doing. Accepting means loving one's partner enough to allow that other person to think and feel and fear and dream things that you are not necessarily comfortable with or may even disagree with. To understand this kind of loving is to begin to grasp how God loves sinners as much as God loves saints!

Acceptance is very much like the special kind of loving that Saint Paul talks about when he says, ''Love is patient, love is kind. It is not jealous, [love] is not pompous, it is not inflated, it is not rude, it does not seek its own interests, it is not quick-tempered, it does not brood over injury. . . . It bears all things, believes all things, hopes all things, endures all things'' (1 Corinthians 13:4-7). Paul instructed the Christians of his day that this sort of accepting love is one of the special ''spiritual gifts'' that comes to us from the Holy Spirit (see 1 Corinthians 12:1-11).

Wise Christian couples thank God for this gift that is freely available to them, and they patiently work to make it part of their everyday lives. It is truly a God-given skill for problem-solving, personal growth, deeper bonding, and for seeking reconciliation for hurts done to each other.

The following questions are intended to help clarify the important concept of accepting the different thoughts and feelings of one's partner. Take some time to answer these questions on your own, and then discuss them with your partner.

1. What are some examples of accepting the other person, even though we have very different feelings about a particular issue? _____

_____

2. When accepting the thoughts and feelings of my partner causes me to feel uncomfortable, I intend to deal with this by

_____

3. How do I expect my partner to react when things that I say, do, or feel are hard for my partner to accept? _____

_____

Skill #4 — Speaking My Mind and Heart With Love

(Directions: The engaged couple and the sponsor couple should read the information on this page. They should discuss any ideas that need clarification before answering the questions that follow.)

The fourth skill, "speaking my mind and heart with love," is similar to the first skill, "sharing." The fourth skill builds on what we have already "shared" and "heard" and "accepted." It takes the further step of speaking about issues and needs and hopes and dreams that are likely to be difficult to deal with. While acceptance (skill three) could seem to mean that we are committed to the status quo or that we have agreed to never want any changes, this fourth skill of effective communication — "speaking my mind and heart with love" — is a tool for helping a couple continue on a path of change and growth that leads to deeper love and a fuller married life.

It does not work to have "peace at all costs" or always to put my needs second to those of my partner. For example, when I understand my spouse's need for financial security, it may be difficult for me to talk about my desire to buy something that will use up the greater portion of our savings. But I still have to speak the feelings of my heart and the thoughts of my mind with love. Or when I know that my spouse has little interest in personal spiritual development, it may be

hard to talk about my yearning to go to church regularly. Or if it is more and more obvious that my spouse has a problem with alcohol, it may be hard to take the step of intervention. Or it may be that I have a need for more intimate time and sharing with my spouse, but I hesitate to tell my spouse for fear that I may be rejected or misunderstood.

There is a fear of "rocking the boat." But when this happens, the relationship begins to deteriorate. Like a healthy plant encased in a protective coating of plastic, it may continue to look good, but since it cannot grow, it dies.

The skill of "speaking my mind and heart with love" is a tool for ensuring the continuing growth of the relationship. A healthy marriage, like a healthy plant, is always changing and growing into something more and better than it used to be!!

The following questions are intended to help clarify the important concept of speaking one's mind and heart with love. Take some time to answer these questions on your own, and then discuss them with your partner.

1. Give examples of "speaking my mind and heart with love" that have happened in your current relationship and indicate how both of you felt before, during, and after this kind of sharing. _____

_____

2. Explain how you and your partner will take steps to work toward continual growth rather than settling for security and stability. _____

_____

3. Consider the statement: "The longer the relationship, the more difficult it is to risk the vulnerability of communication." Agree or disagree and give your reasons. _____

_____

The Value of Effective Communication

(Directions: The engaged couple and the sponsor couple should read the information on this page. They should discuss any ideas that need clarification before answering the questions that follow.)

When two people are truly "in love," they open the boundaries of their personal identities and let another person into the most intimate areas of their private selves. People in love can become so united that they think the same thoughts, like the same foods, and desire always to be together. When one person cries, the other tastes the salt of the tears!

For two people in love, the experience of togetherness can become much more important than one's personal identity. This deep union does have its advantages. It can feel cozy, protective, and secure. But it also has its limitations and can inhibit personal growth and individual choice. If lovers are going to continue growing as persons, it is necessary to be separate individuals as well as close companions.

A couple can achieve the proper balance between closeness and separateness in a relationship by developing effective communication methods. This does not come naturally, however, and what they have learned in the past may not be correct. Ideas about marital communication often come from the experiences of communicating with members of one's family of origin (parents, grandparents, brothers and sisters). This can present a problem since so many families and so many married couples have rather poor patterns of communication. Families of origin teach things like, "It is best not to talk about problems because it only makes them worse." They imply that "women have feelings and are emotional, but real men are those who do not let their emotions show." Family members come to believe that there are all sorts of things that are simply "not talked about." They also foster the myth that "if you really love me, you know what I want without me having to tell you."

Poor communication is a major factor in marital problems. Effective communication, on the other hand, can promote personal growth and maturity as well as mutual harmony. Every couple can learn to communicate more effectively. In improving one's communication skills, the first step is often the hardest. It involves admitting that there is a lot more to learn about each other than what is known from being "in love." The second step calls for recognizing that many of the communication patterns learned during one's growing up years may *not* be helpful patterns of behavior. The third step calls for couples to learn and practice some new skills.

The four major skills needed for effective marital communication are:

1. sharing my own inner thoughts and feelings;
2. hearing what the other has to share;
3. accepting myself and my spouse;
4. speaking my mind and heart with love.

This evening's questions and experiences are designed to help you learn and practice these four skills.

Questions for Private Reflection and Dialogue:
Learning to Share and Hear About Our Differences

Skill #1 — Sharing. In writing your responses to these questions, try to share your inner thoughts and feelings as honestly as you can. Focus on your own personal experience by using "I messages" as much as possible (rather than writing about "you"). There is a special value in sharing your feelings rather than merely your opinions or theories.

Skill #2 — Listening. When you share what you have written, try to really listen to what the other person is saying. Resist the urge to react to or argue about what the other person is sharing. The best response is: "Tell me more about what you are feeling so that I can understand you more clearly."

1. How is my personality different from my partner's? _____
_____

2. The personality trait of my partner that I most admire is _____. The personality trait of my partner that I find difficult to tolerate and difficult to talk about is _____

3. In what ways are we an example of "opposites attract" and how do I feel about this? _____
_____

4. Recall a recent disagreement. Did it have anything to do with different assumptions or expectations, and how did we resolve it? _____

_____

5. What is a potential disagreement that is *likely* to happen in the future? _____

_____

6. My ideas about God, church, or religion are somewhat different from my partner's because I believe that _____

_____

7. What disagreements will arise over religion and how do I intend to deal with them? _____

_____

8. I admit that I do too much (smoking, working, playing, drinking alcohol, TV watching, complaining, arguing, pouting, spending time with friends, and so forth) _____

_____

My partner's excessive behaviors include _____

_____

I intend to deal with this by _____

_____

9. Toward my future in-laws, I feel _____

_____

My partner responds to this by _____

_____

10. Other than my partner, who is the person I confide in the most? _____ What does my partner think about my confiding in this person? _____

_____

11. Can I imagine sharing things with that person which I might not share with my partner? _____
How will this affect my relationship with my partner? _____

_____

12. The way we handled disagreements/problems in my family while I was growing up was
(Check the ones that best fit your family.)
    A. [ ] Avoidance. Problems were simply not talked about.
    B. [ ] Physical/verbal violence. Destructive fighting.
    C. [ ] Passivity. We ignored and denied our problems.
    D. [ ] Giving in. The most powerful always "won."
    E. [ ] Pouting. A way of warning others to stay away.
    F. [ ] Yelling and screaming. A way of punishing others.
    G. [ ] Withdrawal. Hiding from problems and disagreement.
    H. [ ] Manipulation. Covering conflict with gifts or promises.
    I. [ ] Compromise. We learned to give and take.
    J. [ ] Collaboration. We worked together for what was best.

13. At the present time, how are my partner and I dealing with differences and conflicts?
(Check the ones that are appropriate.)
    A. [ ] Avoidance. Problems are simply not talked about.
    B. [ ] Physical/verbal violence. Destructive fighting.
    C. [ ] Passivity. We ignore and deny our problems.
    D. [ ] Giving in. The most powerful "wins."
    E. [ ] Pouting. A way of warning others to stay away.

F. [ ] Yelling and screaming. A way of punishing others.

G. [ ] Withdrawal. Hiding from problems and conflict.

H. [ ] Manipulation. We cover conflict with gifts or promises.

I. [ ] Compromise. We have learned to give and take.

J. [ ] Collaboration. We work together for what is best.

14. Why am I comfortable/not comfortable (circle one) with our present method(s) of dealing with disagreements? _____

_____

15. I want my partner and I to deal with disagreements by _____

_____

_____

16. Some guidelines that would help us be more successful in conflict resolution include _____

_____

Skill #3 — The Special Skill and Gift of Mutual Acceptance

(Directions: The engaged couple and the sponsor couple should read the information below. They should discuss any ideas that need clarification before answering the questions that follow.)

The third major skill of effective marital communication involves accepting the uniqueness of one another. In the language of marital communication, accepting goes beyond the standard dictionary definition of the word. The dictionary says that accepting means "to receive willingly" or "to agree with" or "to give approval." Sometimes it is easy to "accept" in this way what your partner has to share about himself or herself. It is not as easy to accept thoughts and feelings and actions that you disagree with.

The accepting in this case calls for a decision to treasure and value the person (my spouse or myself) and resist the urge to reject or condemn the person as bad or evil because of what he or she is thinking or feeling or hoping or fearing or doing. Accepting means loving one's partner enough to allow that other person to think and feel and fear and dream things that you are not necessarily comfortable with or may even disagree with. To understand this kind of loving is to begin to grasp how God loves sinners as much as God loves saints!

Acceptance is very much like the special kind of loving that Saint Paul talks about when he says, "Love is patient, love is kind. It is not jealous, [love] is not pompous, it is not inflated, it is not rude, it does not seek its own interests, it is not quick-tempered, it does not brood over injury. . . . It bears all things, believes all things, hopes all things, endures all things" (1 Corinthians 13:4-7). Paul instructed the Christians of his day that this sort of accepting love is one of the special "spiritual gifts" that comes to us from the Holy Spirit (see 1 Corinthians 12:1-11).

Wise Christian couples thank God for this gift that is freely available to them, and they patiently work to make it part of their everyday lives. It is truly a God-given skill for problem-solving, personal growth, deeper bonding, and for seeking reconciliation for hurts done to each other.

The following questions are intended to help clarify the important concept of accepting the different thoughts and feelings of one's partner. Take some time to answer these questions on your own, and then discuss them with your partner.

1. What are some examples of accepting the other person, even though we have very different feelings about a particular issue? _____

_____

2. When accepting the thoughts and feelings of my partner causes me to feel uncomfortable, I intend to deal with this by _____

_____

3. How do I expect my partner to react when things that I say, do, or feel are hard for my partner to accept? _____

_____

Skill #4 — Speaking My Mind and Heart With Love

(Directions: The engaged couple and the sponsor couple should read the information on this page. They should discuss any ideas that need clarification before answering the questions that follow.)

The fourth skill, "speaking my mind and heart with love," is similar to the first skill, "sharing." The fourth skill builds on what we have already "shared" and "heard" and "accepted." It takes the further step of speaking about issues and needs and hopes and dreams that are likely to be difficult to deal with. While acceptance (skill three) could seem to mean that we are committed to the status quo or that we have agreed to never want any changes, this fourth skill of effective communication — "speaking my mind and heart with love" — is a tool for helping a couple continue on a path of change and growth that leads to deeper love and a fuller married life.

It does not work to have "peace at all costs" or always to put my needs second to those of my partner. For example, when I understand my spouse's need for financial security, it may be difficult for me to talk about my desire to buy something that will use up the greater portion of our savings. But I still have to speak the feelings of my heart and the thoughts of my mind with love. Or when I know that my spouse has little interest in personal spiritual development, it may be hard to talk about my yearning to go to church regularly. Or if it is more and more obvious that my spouse has a problem with alcohol, it may be hard to take the step of intervention. Or it may be that I have a need for more intimate time and sharing with my spouse, but I hesitate to tell my spouse for fear that I may be rejected or misunderstood.

There is a fear of "rocking the boat." But when this happens, the relationship begins to deteriorate. Like a healthy plant encased in a protective coating of plastic, it may continue to look good, but since it cannot grow, it dies.

The skill of "speaking my mind and heart with love" is a tool for ensuring the continuing growth of the relationship. A healthy marriage, like a healthy plant, is always changing and growing into something more and better than it used to be!!

The following questions are intended to help clarify the important concept of speaking one's mind and heart with love. Take some time to answer these questions on your own, and then discuss them with your partner.

1. Give examples of "speaking my mind and heart with love" that have happened in your current relationship and indicate how both of you felt before, during, and after this kind of sharing. _____

_____

2. Explain how you and your partner will take steps to work toward continual growth rather than settling for security and stability. _____

_____

3. Consider the statement: "The longer the relationship, the more difficult it is to risk the vulnerability of communication." Agree or disagree and give your reasons. _____

_____

The Value of Effective Communication

(Directions: The engaged couple and the sponsor couple should read the information on this page. They should discuss any ideas that need clarification before answering the questions that follow.)

When two people are truly "in love," they open the boundaries of their personal identities and let another person into the most intimate areas of their private selves. People in love can become so united that they think the same thoughts, like the same foods, and desire always to be together. When one person cries, the other tastes the salt of the tears!

For two people in love, the experience of togetherness can become much more important than one's personal identity. This deep union does have its advantages. It can feel cozy, protective, and secure. But it also has its limitations and can inhibit personal growth and individual choice. If lovers are going to continue growing as persons, it is necessary to be separate individuals as well as close companions.

A couple can achieve the proper balance between closeness and separateness in a relationship by developing effective communication methods. This does not come naturally, however, and what they have learned in the past may not be correct. Ideas about marital communication often come from the experiences of communicating with members of one's family of origin (parents, grandparents, brothers and sisters). This can present a problem since so many families and so many married couples have rather poor patterns of communication. Families of origin teach things like, "It is best not to talk about problems because it only makes them worse." They imply that "women have feelings and are emotional, but real men are those who do not let their emotions show." Family members come to believe that there are all sorts of things that are simply "not talked about." They also foster the myth that "if you really love me, you know what I want without me having to tell you."

Poor communication is a major factor in marital problems. Effective communication, on the other hand, can promote personal growth and maturity as well as mutual harmony. Every couple can learn to communicate more effectively. In improving one's communication skills, the first step is often the hardest. It involves admitting that there is a lot more to learn about each other than what is known from being "in love." The second step calls for recognizing that many of the communication patterns learned during one's growing up years may *not* be helpful patterns of behavior. The third step calls for couples to learn and practice some new skills.

The four major skills needed for effective marital communication are:
1. sharing my own inner thoughts and feelings;
2. hearing what the other has to share;
3. accepting myself and my spouse;
4. speaking my mind and heart with love.

This evening's questions and experiences are designed to help you learn and practice these four skills.

Questions for Private Reflection and Dialogue:
Learning to Share and Hear About Our Differences

Skill #1 — Sharing. In writing your responses to these questions, try to share your inner thoughts and feelings as honestly as you can. Focus on your own personal experience by using "I messages" as much as possible (rather than writing about "you"). There is a special value in sharing your feelings rather than merely your opinions or theories.

Skill #2 — Listening. When you share what you have written, try to really listen to what the other person is saying. Resist the urge to react to or argue about what the other person is sharing. The best response is: "Tell me more about what you are feeling so that I can understand you more clearly."

1. How is my personality different from my partner's? _____
_____

2. The personality trait of my partner that I most admire is _____. The personality trait of my partner that I find difficult to tolerate and difficult to talk about is _____

3. In what ways are we an example of "opposites attract" and how do I feel about this? _____
_____

4. Recall a recent disagreement. Did it have anything to do with different assumptions or expectations, and how did we resolve it? _____

_____

5. What is a potential disagreement that is *likely* to happen in the future? _____

_____

6. My ideas about God, church, or religion are somewhat different from my partner's because I believe that _____

_____

7. What disagreements will arise over religion and how do I intend to deal with them? _____

_____

8. I admit that I do too much (smoking, working, playing, drinking alcohol, TV watching, complaining, arguing, pouting, spending time with friends, and so forth)_____

_____

My partner's excessive behaviors include _____

_____

I intend to deal with this by _____

_____

9. Toward my future in-laws, I feel _____

_____

My partner responds to this by _____

_____

10. Other than my partner, who is the person I confide in the most? _____ What does my partner think about my confiding in this person? _____

_____

11. Can I imagine sharing things with that person which I might not share with my partner? _____

How will this affect my relationship with my partner? _____

_____

12. The way we handled disagreements/problems in my family while I was growing up was
(Check the ones that best fit your family.)
   A. [ ] Avoidance. Problems were simply not talked about.
   B. [ ] Physical/verbal violence. Destructive fighting.
   C. [ ] Passivity. We ignored and denied our problems.
   D. [ ] Giving in. The most powerful always ''won.''
   E. [ ] Pouting. A way of warning others to stay away.
   F. [ ] Yelling and screaming. A way of punishing others.
   G. [ ] Withdrawal. Hiding from problems and disagreement.
   H. [ ] Manipulation. Covering conflict with gifts or promises.
   I. [ ] Compromise. We learned to give and take.
   J. [ ] Collaboration. We worked together for what was best.
13. At the present time, how are my partner and I dealing with differences and conflicts?
(Check the ones that are appropriate.)
   A. [ ] Avoidance. Problems are simply not talked about.
   B. [ ] Physical/verbal violence. Destructive fighting.
   C. [ ] Passivity. We ignore and deny our problems.
   D. [ ] Giving in. The most powerful ''wins.''
   E. [ ] Pouting. A way of warning others to stay away.

F. [ ] Yelling and screaming. A way of punishing others.

G. [ ] Withdrawal. Hiding from problems and conflict.

H. [ ] Manipulation. We cover conflict with gifts or promises.

I. [ ] Compromise. We have learned to give and take.

J. [ ] Collaboration. We work together for what is best.

14. Why am I comfortable/not comfortable (circle one) with our present method(s) of dealing with disagreements? _____

_____

15. I want my partner and I to deal with disagreements by _____

_____

_____

16. Some guidelines that would help us be more successful in conflict resolution include _____

_____

Skill #3 — The Special Skill and Gift of Mutual Acceptance

(Directions: The engaged couple and the sponsor couple should read the information below. They should discuss any ideas that need clarification before answering the questions that follow.)

The third major skill of effective marital communication involves accepting the uniqueness of one another. In the language of marital communication, accepting goes beyond the standard dictionary definition of the word. The dictionary says that accepting means "to receive willingly" or "to agree with" or "to give approval." Sometimes it is easy to "accept" in this way what your partner has to share about himself or herself. It is not as easy to accept thoughts and feelings and actions that you disagree with.

The accepting in this case calls for a decision to treasure and value the person (my spouse or myself) and resist the urge to reject or condemn the person as bad or evil because of what he or she is thinking or feeling or hoping or fearing or doing. Accepting means loving one's partner enough to allow that other person to think and feel and fear and dream things that you are not necessarily comfortable with or may even disagree with. To understand this kind of loving is to begin to grasp how God loves sinners as much as God loves saints!

Acceptance is very much like the special kind of

loving that Saint Paul talks about when he says, "Love is patient, love is kind. It is not jealous, [love] is not pompous, it is not inflated, it is not rude, it does not seek its own interests, it is not quick-tempered, it does not brood over injury. . . . It bears all things, believes all things, hopes all things, endures all things" (1 Corinthians 13:4-7). Paul instructed the Christians of his day that this sort of accepting love is one of the special "spiritual gifts" that comes to us from the Holy Spirit (see 1 Corinthians 12:1-11).

Wise Christian couples thank God for this gift that is freely available to them, and they patiently work to make it part of their everyday lives. It is truly a God-given skill for problem-solving, personal growth, deeper bonding, and for seeking reconciliation for hurts done to each other.

The following questions are intended to help clarify the important concept of accepting the different thoughts and feelings of one's partner. Take some time to answer these questions on your own, and then discuss them with your partner.

1. What are some examples of accepting the other person, even though we have very different feelings about a particular issue? _____

_____

2. When accepting the thoughts and feelings of my partner causes me to feel uncomfortable, I intend to deal with this by

_____ .

_____

3. How do I expect my partner to react when things that I say, do, or feel are hard for my partner to accept? _____

_____

Skill #4 — Speaking My Mind and Heart With Love

(Directions: The engaged couple and the sponsor couple should read the information on this page. They should discuss any ideas that need clarification before answering the questions that follow.)

The fourth skill, "speaking my mind and heart with love," is similar to the first skill, "sharing." The fourth skill builds on what we have already "shared" and "heard" and "accepted." It takes the further step of speaking about issues and needs and hopes and dreams that are likely to be difficult to deal with. While acceptance (skill three) could seem to mean that we are committed to the status quo or that we have agreed to never want any changes, this fourth skill of effective communication — "speaking my mind and heart with love" — is a tool for helping a couple continue on a path of change and growth that leads to deeper love and a fuller married life.

It does not work to have "peace at all costs" or always to put my needs second to those of my partner. For example, when I understand my spouse's need for financial security, it may be difficult for me to talk about my desire to buy something that will use up the greater portion of our savings. But I still have to speak the feelings of my heart and the thoughts of my mind with love. Or when I know that my spouse has little interest in personal spiritual development, it may be hard to talk about my yearning to go to church regularly. Or if it is more and more obvious that my spouse has a problem with alcohol, it may be hard to take the step of intervention. Or it may be that I have a need for more intimate time and sharing with my spouse, but I hesitate to tell my spouse for fear that I may be rejected or misunderstood.

There is a fear of "rocking the boat." But when this happens, the relationship begins to deteriorate. Like a healthy plant encased in a protective coating of plastic, it may continue to look good, but since it cannot grow, it dies.

The skill of "speaking my mind and heart with love" is a tool for ensuring the continuing growth of the relationship. A healthy marriage, like a healthy plant, is always changing and growing into something more and better than it used to be!!

The following questions are intended to help clarify the important concept of speaking one's mind and heart with love. Take some time to answer these questions on your own, and then discuss them with your partner.

1. Give examples of "speaking my mind and heart with love" that have happened in your current relationship and indicate how both of you felt before, during, and after this kind of sharing. _____

_____

2. Explain how you and your partner will take steps to work toward continual growth rather than settling for security and stability. _____

_____

3. Consider the statement: "The longer the relationship, the more difficult it is to risk the vulnerability of communication." Agree or disagree and give your reasons. _____

_____

The Value of Effective Communication

(Directions: The engaged couple and the sponsor couple should read the information on this page. They should discuss any ideas that need clarification before answering the questions that follow.)

When two people are truly "in love," they open the boundaries of their personal identities and let another person into the most intimate areas of their private selves. People in love can become so united that they think the same thoughts, like the same foods, and desire always to be together. When one person cries, the other tastes the salt of the tears!

For two people in love, the experience of togetherness can become much more important than one's personal identity. This deep union does have its advantages. It can feel cozy, protective, and secure. But it also has its limitations and can inhibit personal growth and individual choice. If lovers are going to continue growing as persons, it is necessary to be separate individuals as well as close companions.

A couple can achieve the proper balance between closeness and separateness in a relationship by developing effective communication methods. This does not come naturally, however, and what they have learned in the past may not be correct. Ideas about marital communication often come from the experiences of communicating with members of one's family of origin (parents, grandparents, brothers and sisters). This can present a problem since so many families and so many married couples have rather poor patterns of communication. Families of origin teach things like, "It is best not to talk about problems because it only makes them worse." They imply that "women have feelings and are emotional, but real men are those who do not let their emotions show." Family members come to believe that there are all sorts of things that are simply "not talked about." They also foster the myth that "if you really love me, you know what I want without me having to tell you."

Poor communication is a major factor in marital problems. Effective communication, on the other hand, can promote personal growth and maturity as well as mutual harmony. Every couple can learn to communicate more effectively. In improving one's communication skills, the first step is often the hardest. It involves admitting that there is a lot more to learn about each other than what is known from being "in love." The second step calls for recognizing that many of the communication patterns learned during one's growing up years may *not* be helpful patterns of behavior. The third step calls for couples to learn and practice some new skills.

The four major skills needed for effective marital communication are:

1. sharing my own inner thoughts and feelings;
2. hearing what the other has to share;
3. accepting myself and my spouse;
4. speaking my mind and heart with love.

This evening's questions and experiences are designed to help you learn and practice these four skills.

Questions for Private Reflection and Dialogue:
Learning to Share and Hear About Our Differences

Skill #1 — Sharing. In writing your responses to these questions, try to share your inner thoughts and feelings as honestly as you can. Focus on your own personal experience by using "I messages" as much as possible (rather than writing about "you"). There is a special value in sharing your feelings rather than merely your opinions or theories.

Skill #2 — Listening. When you share what you have written, try to really listen to what the other person is saying. Resist the urge to react to or argue about what the other person is sharing. The best response is: "Tell me more about what you are feeling so that I can understand you more clearly."

1. How is my personality different from my partner's? _____

_____

2. The personality trait of my partner that I most admire is _____. The personality trait of my partner that I find difficult to tolerate and difficult to talk about is _____

3. In what ways are we an example of "opposites attract" and how do I feel about this? _____

_____

4. Recall a recent disagreement. Did it have anything to do with different assumptions or expectations, and how did we resolve it? _____

_____

5. What is a potential disagreement that is *likely* to happen in the future? _____

_____

6. My ideas about God, church, or religion are somewhat different from my partner's because I believe that _____

_____

7. What disagreements will arise over religion and how do I intend to deal with them? _____

_____

8. I admit that I do too much (smoking, working, playing, drinking alcohol, TV watching, complaining, arguing, pouting, spending time with friends, and so forth) _____

_____

My partner's excessive behaviors include _____

_____

I intend to deal with this by _____

_____

9. Toward my future in-laws, I feel _____

_____

My partner responds to this by _____

_____

10. Other than my partner, who is the person I confide in the most? _____ What does my partner think about my confiding in this person? _____

_____

11. Can I imagine sharing things with that person which I might not share with my partner? _____

How will this affect my relationship with my partner? _____

_____

12. The way we handled disagreements/problems in my family while I was growing up was
(Check the ones that best fit your family.)
   A. [ ] Avoidance. Problems were simply not talked about.
   B. [ ] Physical/verbal violence. Destructive fighting.
   C. [ ] Passivity. We ignored and denied our problems.
   D. [ ] Giving in. The most powerful always "won."
   E. [ ] Pouting. A way of warning others to stay away.
   F. [ ] Yelling and screaming. A way of punishing others.
   G. [ ] Withdrawal. Hiding from problems and disagreement.
   H. [ ] Manipulation. Covering conflict with gifts or promises.
   I. [ ] Compromise. We learned to give and take.
   J. [ ] Collaboration. We worked together for what was best.

13. At the present time, how are my partner and I dealing with differences and conflicts?
(Check the ones that are appropriate.)
   A. [ ] Avoidance. Problems are simply not talked about.
   B. [ ] Physical/verbal violence. Destructive fighting.
   C. [ ] Passivity. We ignore and deny our problems.
   D. [ ] Giving in. The most powerful "wins."
   E. [ ] Pouting. A way of warning others to stay away.

F. [ ] Yelling and screaming. A way of punishing others.

G. [ ] Withdrawal. Hiding from problems and conflict.

H. [ ] Manipulation. We cover conflict with gifts or promises.

I. [ ] Compromise. We have learned to give and take.

J. [ ] Collaboration. We work together for what is best.

14. Why am I comfortable/not comfortable (circle one) with our present method(s) of dealing with disagreements? _____

_____

15. I want my partner and I to deal with disagreements by _____

_____

_____

16. Some guidelines that would help us be more successful in conflict resolution include _____

_____

Skill #3 — The Special Skill and Gift of Mutual Acceptance

(Directions: The engaged couple and the sponsor couple should read the information below. They should discuss any ideas that need clarification before answering the questions that follow.)

The third major skill of effective marital communication involves accepting the uniqueness of one another. In the language of marital communication, accepting goes beyond the standard dictionary definition of the word. The dictionary says that accepting means "to receive willingly" or "to agree with" or "to give approval." Sometimes it is easy to "accept" in this way what your partner has to share about himself or herself. It is not as easy to accept thoughts and feelings and actions that you disagree with.

The accepting in this case calls for a decision to treasure and value the person (my spouse or myself) and resist the urge to reject or condemn the person as bad or evil because of what he or she is thinking or feeling or hoping or fearing or doing. Accepting means loving one's partner enough to allow that other person to think and feel and fear and dream things that you are not necessarily comfortable with or may even disagree with. To understand this kind of loving is to begin to grasp how God loves sinners as much as God loves saints!

Acceptance is very much like the special kind of loving that Saint Paul talks about when he says, "Love is patient, love is kind. It is not jealous, [love] is not pompous, it is not inflated, it is not rude, it does not seek its own interests, it is not quick-tempered, it does not brood over injury. . . . It bears all things, believes all things, hopes all things, endures all things" (1 Corinthians 13:4-7). Paul instructed the Christians of his day that this sort of accepting love is one of the special "spiritual gifts" that comes to us from the Holy Spirit (see 1 Corinthians 12:1-11).

Wise Christian couples thank God for this gift that is freely available to them, and they patiently work to make it part of their everyday lives. It is truly a God-given skill for problem-solving, personal growth, deeper bonding, and for seeking reconciliation for hurts done to each other.

The following questions are intended to help clarify the important concept of accepting the different thoughts and feelings of one's partner. Take some time to answer these questions on your own, and then discuss them with your partner.

1. What are some examples of accepting the other person, even though we have very different feelings about a particular issue? _____

_____

2. When accepting the thoughts and feelings of my partner causes me to feel uncomfortable, I intend to deal with this by _____

_____

3. How do I expect my partner to react when things that I say, do, or feel are hard for my partner to accept? _____

_____

Skill #4 — Speaking My Mind and Heart With Love

(Directions: The engaged couple and the sponsor couple should read the information on this page. They should discuss any ideas that need clarification before answering the questions that follow.)

The fourth skill, "speaking my mind and heart with love," is similar to the first skill, "sharing." The fourth skill builds on what we have already "shared" and "heard" and "accepted." It takes the further step of speaking about issues and needs and hopes and dreams that are likely to be difficult to deal with. While acceptance (skill three) could seem to mean that we are committed to the status quo or that we have agreed to never want any changes, this fourth skill of effective communication — "speaking my mind and heart with love" — is a tool for helping a couple continue on a path of change and growth that leads to deeper love and a fuller married life.

It does not work to have "peace at all costs" or always to put my needs second to those of my partner. For example, when I understand my spouse's need for financial security, it may be difficult for me to talk about my desire to buy something that will use up the greater portion of our savings. But I still have to speak the feelings of my heart and the thoughts of my mind with love. Or when I know that my spouse has little interest in personal spiritual development, it may be hard to talk about my yearning to go to church regularly. Or if it is more and more obvious that my spouse has a problem with alcohol, it may be hard to take the step of intervention. Or it may be that I have a need for more intimate time and sharing with my spouse, but I hesitate to tell my spouse for fear that I may be rejected or misunderstood.

There is a fear of "rocking the boat." But when this happens, the relationship begins to deteriorate. Like a healthy plant encased in a protective coating of plastic, it may continue to look good, but since it cannot grow, it dies.

The skill of "speaking my mind and heart with love" is a tool for ensuring the continuing growth of the relationship. A healthy marriage, like a healthy plant, is always changing and growing into something more and better than it used to be!!

The following questions are intended to help clarify the important concept of speaking one's mind and heart with love. Take some time to answer these questions on your own, and then discuss them with your partner.

1. Give examples of "speaking my mind and heart with love" that have happened in your current relationship and indicate how both of you felt before, during, and after this kind of sharing. ——

2. Explain how you and your partner will take steps to work toward continual growth rather than settling for security and stability. ——

3. Consider the statement: "The longer the relationship, the more difficult it is to risk the vulnerability of communication." Agree or disagree and give your reasons. ——

EVENING **4**

Marriage Is Intimate

Opening Prayer

A reading from the First Letter to the Corinthians 13:1-13.

If I speak in human and angelic tongues but do not have love, I am a resounding gong or a clashing cymbal. And if I have the gift of prophecy and comprehend all mysteries and all knowledge; if I have all faith so as to move mountains, but do not have love, I am nothing. If I give away everything I own, and if I hand my body over so that I may boast but do not have love, I gain nothing.

Love is patient, love is kind. It is not jealous, [love] is not pompous, it is not inflated, it is not rude, it does not seek its own interests, it is not quick-tempered, it does not brood over injury, it does not rejoice over wrongdoing but rejoices with the truth. It bears all things, believes all things, hopes all things, endures all things.

Love never fails. If there are prophecies, they will be brought to nothing; if tongues, they will cease; if knowledge, it will be brought to nothing. For we know partially and we prophesy partially, but when the perfect comes, the partial will pass away. When I was a child, I used to talk as a child, think as a child, reason as a child; when I became a man, I put aside childish things. At present we see indistinctly, as in a mirror, but then face to face. At present I know partially; then I shall know fully, as I am fully known. So faith, hope, love remain, these three; but the greatest of these is love.

The sponsor couple reads aloud the following prayer:

Lord God, please give us the wisdom to keep thanking you for these gifts that you so willingly keep on giving. We thank you for: *Faith* in one another that goes deeper than what we can see with our eyes; *Hope* that empowers us to trust one another during the hard times; *Love* that motivates us to be ever faithful to our commitment to be lovers. Amen.

Closing Prayer

The engaged couple reads aloud the following prayer:

Lord, you are the God who is love. Married love is meant to be experienced as a sharing in your own love. Help us learn to be like you in expressing our love for one another.

You are a passionate and yet tender lover. Help us to be full of passion and tenderness in touching and embracing one another.

As you gave your own Son a body to be given in sacrifice for others, so you have given us the ability to give our bodies to one another in love that is precious and life-giving. Help us to see in this special gift of mutual self-giving a sign of the total giving of our selves . . . our hearts, our minds, our spirits, as well as our bodies to one another. Amen.

Intimacy...An Essential Element of Christian Marriage

(Directions: The engaged couple and the sponsor couple should read the information on this page. They should discuss any ideas that need clarification before answering the questions that follow.)

Intimacy is a word that has many levels of meaning. For most people in our culture, intimacy suggests physical, even genital closeness. We hear, for example, that a friend is being intimate with her boyfriend; or we read in the newspaper about a sale on intimate apparel.

It is also important to reflect upon what we learned in our family of origin about intimacy. For many of us, intimate also meant "secret" and something "not to be discussed" with the children or even with one's spouse.

When we speak of intimacy in Christian marriage, however, we are not talking about something secretive. We are talking about a kind of mutual sharing that is physical, emotional, intellectual, and spiritual. Christian marriage is intimate when spouses share their thoughts, their feelings, their hopes, their dreams, their fears, their spirituality, their possessions, their responsibilities, their families, and also their physical selves with one another. When spouses share every part of their lives, they are truly being intimate. It calls for a *total* sharing of one's person that respects and maintains the individual identity of both persons. In much the same way that Jesus and God are one, so Christian spouses become collaborative partners yet remain unique individuals (see John 17:21).

The "intimacy" of Christian marriage is difficult because it requires vulnerability. Vulnerability involves risk and even fear. The experience of Christians through the centuries is that our relationship with God encourages us to be intimate with one another. God's love for us makes us more alive rather than less alive; God's love for us makes us more free to be who we choose to be. Wise spouses know they can depend on the strength and power of God to help them risk deeper and deeper openness and intimacy with one another. They remember that "there is no fear in love, but perfect love drives out fear because fear has to do with punishment, and so one who fears is not yet perfect in love" (1 John 4:18).

Questions for Reflection and Dialogue

1. How did I experience intimacy in my family of origin? _____
_____

2. What does intimacy mean to me today? _____
_____

3. One aspect of intimacy involves the willingness to share my inner feelings with my spouse. Which feelings do I think I will find it difficult to share with my partner? (Check all that apply.)

A. [ ] bored	**F.** [ ] tender	**K.** [ ] joyful	**P.** [ ] sexually aroused
B. [ ] excited	**G.** [ ] angry	**L.** [ ] guilty	**Q.** [ ] distant
C. [ ] frustrated	**H.** [ ] afraid	**M.** [ ] anxious	**R.** [ ] isolated
D. [ ] jealous	**I.** [ ] ashamed	**N.** [ ] sad	**S.** [ ] close
E. [ ] embarrassed	**J.** [ ] lonely	**O.** [ ] silly	**T.** [ ] supported

4. What are my feelings about making a commitment to give of my "whole person" (thoughts, feelings, possessions, hopes, dreams, fears, and so forth) to my partner for a lifetime? _____
_____

5. What are several specific and practical things we can do to help us be more intimate as a Christian married couple? _____
_____

6. How does the intimacy of Christian marriage promote and encourage greater self-identity? _____
_____

(Directions: After answering the previous six questions, the couples should read the section below entitled "A Christian Vision of Sexuality, Marriage, and Parenthood" before answering questions 7-20. The sharing time with your partner and between the two couples will include questions 1-20.)

A Christian Vision of Sexuality, Marriage, and Parenthood

(Directions: The engaged couple and the sponsor couple should read the information on this page. They should discuss any ideas that need clarification before answering the questions that follow.)

Marriage is intended to be a way of life in which spouses strive to give themselves totally as a gift to one another at every level of their being. While sexuality is only one dimension of Christian marriage, it is necessary to pay particular attention to this topic because there are such contradictory views about the meaning of sexuality and sexual intercourse.

History is filled with examples of incorrect biological information leading to confused sociological and theological understandings of sexual intercourse and marital sexuality. Modern science has helped us see human sexuality and the processes of fertility much more accurately. Yet science can only tell us about the biology and physiology of sexuality and sexual intercourse. The *meaning* of sexuality and sexual intercourse comes from the fields of philosophy and religion. In today's society, however, there are many religions and philosophies teaching very different messages about the meaning of sexuality and sexual intercourse. This can cause confusion for engaged and married couples. Further confusion comes from inadequate sexual education and from the misinformation and hedonistic values espoused by TV, music, and advertising.

Most families, it seems, have done a poor job of sharing accurate information and Christian values and attitudes about sexuality and sexual intercourse. This is a primary reason that most "good Christians" do not really understand or live the Christian ideas and attitudes about sexuality and sexual intercourse. But, lest we be too hard on our parents, it is useful to remember that they, in turn, received poor information from their own parents.

It is more difficult to gauge accurately the impact of modern media on our values, attitudes, and expectations. Some people argue that the media merely reflect what is already going on, rather than actually making things happen. But there is little doubt that advertising uses both women and men as sex objects to sell products. In TV and movies, the "giving and receiving of the whole person" in marriage is often rejected as naïve. "Living together" is promoted as a wise option to marriage. Human fertility is viewed as an inconvenience to be avoided by using artificial contraception, rather than as a special gift of God to be shared with one's spouse.

Where do we find useful information that Christian couples can use in the development of a healthy Christian marriage?

A good starting point for reviewing our ideas about sexuality and sexual intercourse is the Bible. The Book of Genesis specifically describes the Lord God as creating human beings male and female and directing them to be fertile and multiply. The Creator offers this explanation: "It is not good for the man to be alone. I will make a suitable partner for him." To make sure we do not miss the point, the Lord God looks at the whole created universe — including humankind and sexuality — and says: "It is very good" (see Genesis 1:26–2:18).

Christianity promotes a vision of sexuality that (a) acknowledges the good and positive value of human sexuality, marital intimacy, and sexual intercourse; (b) affirms sexual intercourse as a special sign of permanent and total *marital* commitment; (c) teaches that there is a clear connection between the "lovemaking" and the "childbearing" dimensions of sexual intercourse; and (d) views fertility as a unique participation in the creative power of God.

Questions About Lovemaking, Fertility, and Parenthood

(Directions: These questions are for the engaged couple. The sponsor couple has slightly different questions. After each person has answered the questions on his or her page, the four people should share their responses.)

7. When and where and from whom did I first learn the biological facts about sexual intercourse and what were my feelings about learning this information? _____

8. When and where and from whom did I first learn the *meaning* of sexual intercourse and was this consistent with Christian teachings? _____

9. How successfully and appropriately do I incorporate physical expressions of affection into my relationships with my parents, other members of my family, male and female friends? Explain. _____

10. How well have I incorporated physical expressions of affection into my relationship with my partner? _____

11. Which of these matters concerns me? (Check any that apply to you.)
    A. [ ] I am afraid that I will not be an adequate sex partner.
    B. [ ] I am afraid of getting pregnant.
    C. [ ] I am afraid of appearing ignorant about sex.
    D. [ ] I am worried about not knowing what to do.
    E. [ ] I am afraid that I will find sex to be repulsive.
    F. [ ] I worry about whether either of us has been exposed to AIDS.
    G. [ ] I fear sexual intercourse will bring back bad memories.
    H. [ ] (other) _____

12. How frequently do I expect we will experience sexual intercourse? Explain. _____

13. What can we do to ensure that our experiences of lovemaking will be satisfying for each of us? _____

14. What personal preferences and what differences in male and female sexual response will we need to be aware of in our lovemaking? _____

15. Do I view our fertility more as "gift" or as "problem to deal with"? Explain. _____

16. Are we ready for the possibility of the conception of a child as soon as we are married? _____

(Note: In responding to the following questions about church teaching, answer according to the teaching of your own church. If your partner is of a different denomination, his or her answers may be different from yours.)

17. What does my church teach about "responsible parenthood"? _____

18. What does my church teach about the use of family planning methods? _____

19. What do I understand about "natural family planning" and how does it differ from the "rhythm method"? _____

20. What will we do if we are not able to conceive children because one or both of us are infertile? _____

Intimacy…An Essential Element of Christian Marriage

(Directions: The engaged couple and the sponsor couple should read the information on this page. They should discuss any ideas that need clarification before answering the questions that follow.)

Intimacy is a word that has many levels of meaning. For most people in our culture, intimacy suggests physical, even genital closeness. We hear, for example, that a friend is being intimate with her boyfriend; or we read in the newspaper about a sale on intimate apparel.

It is also important to reflect upon what we learned in our family of origin about intimacy. For many of us, intimate also meant "secret" and something "not to be discussed" with the children or even with one's spouse.

When we speak of intimacy in Christian marriage, however, we are not talking about something secretive. We are talking about a kind of mutual sharing that is physical, emotional, intellectual, and spiritual. Christian marriage is intimate when spouses share their thoughts, their feelings, their hopes, their dreams, their fears, their spirituality, their possessions, their responsibilities, their families, and also their physical selves with one another. When spouses share every part of their lives, they are truly being intimate. It calls for a *total* sharing of one's person that respects and maintains the individual identity of both persons. In much the same way that Jesus and God are one, so Christian spouses become collaborative partners yet remain unique individuals (see John 17:21).

The "intimacy" of Christian marriage is difficult because it requires vulnerability. Vulnerability involves risk and even fear. The experience of Christians through the centuries is that our relationship with God encourages us to be intimate with one another. God's love for us makes us more alive rather than less alive; God's love for us makes us more free to be who we choose to be. Wise spouses know they can depend on the strength and power of God to help them risk deeper and deeper openness and intimacy with one another. They remember that "there is no fear in love, but perfect love drives out fear because fear has to do with punishment, and so one who fears is not yet perfect in love" (1 John 4:18).

Questions for Reflection and Dialogue

1. How did I experience intimacy in my family of origin? _____

_____

2. What does intimacy mean to me today? _____

_____

3. One aspect of intimacy involves the willingness to share my inner feelings with my spouse. Which feelings do I think I will find it difficult to share with my partner? (Check all that apply.)

A. [ ] bored	**F.** [ ] tender	**K.** [ ] joyful	**P.** [ ] sexually aroused
B. [ ] excited	**G.** [ ] angry	**L.** [ ] guilty	**Q.** [ ] distant
C. [ ] frustrated	**H.** [ ] afraid	**M.** [ ] anxious	**R.** [ ] isolated
D. [ ] jealous	**I.** [ ] ashamed	**N.** [ ] sad	**S.** [ ] close
E. [ ] embarrassed	**J.** [ ] lonely	**O.** [ ] silly	**T.** [ ] supported

4. What are my feelings about making a commitment to give of my "whole person" (thoughts, feelings, possessions, hopes, dreams, fears, and so forth) to my partner for a lifetime? _____

_____

5. What are several specific and practical things we can do to help us be more intimate as a Christian married couple? _____

_____

6. How does the intimacy of Christian marriage promote and encourage greater self-identity? _____

_____

(Directions: After answering the previous six questions, the couples should read the section below entitled "A Christian Vision of Sexuality, Marriage, and Parenthood" before answering questions 7-20. The sharing time with your partner and between the two couples will include questions 1-20.)

A Christian Vision of Sexuality, Marriage, and Parenthood

(Directions: The engaged couple and the sponsor couple should read the information on this page. They should discuss any ideas that need clarification before answering the questions that follow.)

Marriage is intended to be a way of life in which spouses strive to give themselves totally as a gift to one another at every level of their being. While sexuality is only one dimension of Christian marriage, it is necessary to pay particular attention to this topic because there are such contradictory views about the meaning of sexuality and sexual intercourse.

History is filled with examples of incorrect biological information leading to confused sociological and theological understandings of sexual intercourse and marital sexuality. Modern science has helped us see human sexuality and the processes of fertility much more accurately. Yet science can only tell us about the biology and physiology of sexuality and sexual intercourse. The *meaning* of sexuality and sexual intercourse comes from the fields of philosophy and religion. In today's society, however, there are many religions and philosophies teaching very different messages about the meaning of sexuality and sexual intercourse. This can cause confusion for engaged and married couples. Further confusion comes from inadequate sexual education and from the misinformation and hedonistic values espoused by TV, music, and advertising.

Most families, it seems, have done a poor job of sharing accurate information and Christian values and attitudes about sexuality and sexual intercourse. This is a primary reason that most "good Christians" do not really understand or live the Christian ideas and attitudes about sexuality and sexual intercourse. But, lest we be too hard on our parents, it is useful to remember that they, in turn, received poor information from their own parents.

It is more difficult to gauge accurately the impact of modern media on our values, attitudes, and expectations. Some people argue that the media merely reflect what is already going on, rather than actually making things happen. But there is little doubt that advertising uses both women and men as sex objects to sell products. In TV and movies, the "giving and receiving of the whole person" in marriage is often rejected as naïve. "Living together" is promoted as a wise option to marriage. Human fertility is viewed as an inconvenience to be avoided by using artificial contraception, rather than as a special gift of God to be shared with one's spouse.

Where do we find useful information that Christian couples can use in the development of a healthy Christian marriage?

A good starting point for reviewing our ideas about sexuality and sexual intercourse is the Bible. The Book of Genesis specifically describes the Lord God as creating human beings male and female and directing them to be fertile and multiply. The Creator offers this explanation: "It is not good for the man to be alone. I will make a suitable partner for him." To make sure we do not miss the point, the Lord God looks at the whole created universe — including humankind and sexuality — and says: "It is very good" (see Genesis 1:26–2:18).

Christianity promotes a vision of sexuality that (a) acknowledges the good and positive value of human sexuality, marital intimacy, and sexual intercourse; (b) affirms sexual intercourse as a special sign of permanent and total *marital* commitment; (c) teaches that there is a clear connection between the "lovemaking" and the "childbearing" dimensions of sexual intercourse; and (d) views fertility as a unique participation in the creative power of God.

Questions About Lovemaking, Fertility, and Parenthood

(Directions: These questions are for the engaged couple. The sponsor couple has slightly different questions. After each person has answered the questions on his or her page, the four people should share their responses.)

7. When and where and from whom did I first learn the biological facts about sexual intercourse and what were my feelings about learning this information? _____

8. When and where and from whom did I first learn the *meaning* of sexual intercourse and was this consistent with Christian teachings? _____

9. How successfully and appropriately do I incorporate physical expressions of affection into my relationships with my parents, other members of my family, male and female friends? Explain. _____

10. How well have I incorporated physical expressions of affection into my relationship with my partner? _____

11. Which of these matters concerns me? (Check any that apply to you.)
    A. [ ] I am afraid that I will not be an adequate sex partner.
    B. [ ] I am afraid of getting pregnant.
    C. [ ] I am afraid of appearing ignorant about sex.
    D. [ ] I am worried about not knowing what to do.
    E. [ ] I am afraid that I will find sex to be repulsive.
    F. [ ] I worry about whether either of us has been exposed to AIDS.
    G. [ ] I fear sexual intercourse will bring back bad memories.
    H. [ ] (other) _____

12. How frequently do I expect we will experience sexual intercourse? Explain. _____

13. What can we do to ensure that our experiences of lovemaking will be satisfying for each of us? _____

14. What personal preferences and what differences in male and female sexual response will we need to be aware of in our lovemaking? _____

15. Do I view our fertility more as ''gift'' or as ''problem to deal with''? Explain. _____

16. Are we ready for the possibility of the conception of a child as soon as we are married? _____

(Note: In responding to the following questions about church teaching, answer according to the teaching of your own church. If your partner is of a different denomination, his or her answers may be different from yours.)

17. What does my church teach about ''responsible parenthood''? _____

18. What does my church teach about the use of family planning methods? _____

19. What do I understand about ''natural family planning'' and how does it differ from the ''rhythm method''? _____

20. What will we do if we are not able to conceive children because one or both of us are infertile? _____

Intimacy...An Essential Element of Christian Marriage

(Directions: The engaged couple and the sponsor couple should read the information on this page. They should discuss any ideas that need clarification before answering the questions that follow.)

Intimacy is a word that has many levels of meaning. For most people in our culture, intimacy suggests physical, even genital closeness. We hear, for example, that a friend is being intimate with her boyfriend; or we read in the newspaper about a sale on intimate apparel.

It is also important to reflect upon what we learned in our family of origin about intimacy. For many of us, intimate also meant "secret" and something "not to be discussed" with the children or even with one's spouse.

When we speak of intimacy in Christian marriage, however, we are not talking about something secretive. We are talking about a kind of mutual sharing that is physical, emotional, intellectual, and spiritual. Christian marriage is intimate when spouses share their thoughts, their feelings, their hopes, their dreams, their fears, their spirituality, their possessions, their responsibilities, their families, and also their physical selves with one another. When spouses share every part of their lives, they are truly

being intimate. It calls for a *total* sharing of one's person that respects and maintains the individual identity of both persons. In much the same way that Jesus and God are one, so Christian spouses become collaborative partners yet remain unique individuals (see John 17:21).

The "intimacy" of Christian marriage is difficult because it requires vulnerability. Vulnerability involves risk and even fear. The experience of Christians through the centuries is that our relationship with God encourages us to be intimate with one another. God's love for us makes us more alive rather than less alive; God's love for us makes us more free to be who we choose to be. Wise spouses know they can depend on the strength and power of God to help them risk deeper and deeper openness and intimacy with one another. They remember that "there is no fear in love, but perfect love drives out fear because fear has to do with punishment, and so one who fears is not yet perfect in love" (1 John 4:18).

Questions for Reflection and Dialogue

1. How did I experience intimacy in my family of origin? _____
_____

2. What does intimacy mean to me today? _____
_____

3. One aspect of intimacy involves the willingness to share my inner feelings with my spouse. Which feelings do I think I will find it difficult to share with my partner? (Check all that apply.)

A. [ ] bored	F. [ ] tender	K. [ ] joyful	P. [ ] sexually aroused
B. [ ] excited	G. [ ] angry	L. [ ] guilty	Q. [ ] distant
C. [ ] frustrated	H. [ ] afraid	M. [ ] anxious	R. [ ] isolated
D. [ ] jealous	I. [ ] ashamed	N. [ ] sad	S. [ ] close
E. [ ] embarrassed	J. [ ] lonely	O. [ ] silly	T. [ ] supported

4. What are my feelings about making a commitment to give of my "whole person" (thoughts, feelings, possessions, hopes, dreams, fears, and so forth) to my partner for a lifetime? _____
_____

5. What are several specific and practical things we can do to help us be more intimate as a Christian married couple? _____
_____

6. How does the intimacy of Christian marriage promote and encourage greater self-identity? _____
_____

(Directions: After answering the previous six questions, the couples should read the section below entitled "A Christian Vision of Sexuality, Marriage, and Parenthood" before answering questions 7-20. The sharing time with your partner and between the two couples will include questions 1-20.)

A Christian Vision of Sexuality, Marriage, and Parenthood

(Directions: The engaged couple and the sponsor couple should read the information on this page. They should discuss any ideas that need clarification before answering the questions that follow.)

Marriage is intended to be a way of life in which spouses strive to give themselves totally as a gift to one another at every level of their being. While sexuality is only one dimension of Christian marriage, it is necessary to pay particular attention to this topic because there are such contradictory views about the meaning of sexuality and sexual intercourse.

History is filled with examples of incorrect biological information leading to confused sociological and theological understandings of sexual intercourse and marital sexuality. Modern science has helped us see human sexuality and the processes of fertility much more accurately. Yet science can only tell us about the biology and physiology of sexuality and sexual intercourse. The *meaning* of sexuality and sexual intercourse comes from the fields of philosophy and religion. In today's society, however, there are many religions and philosophies teaching very different messages about the meaning of sexuality and sexual intercourse. This can cause confusion for engaged and married couples. Further confusion comes from inadequate sexual education and from the misinformation and hedonistic values espoused by TV, music, and advertising.

Most families, it seems, have done a poor job of sharing accurate information and Christian values and attitudes about sexuality and sexual intercourse. This is a primary reason that most "good Christians" do not really understand or live the Christian ideas and attitudes about sexuality and sexual intercourse. But, lest we be too hard on our parents, it is useful to remember that they, in turn, received poor information from their own parents.

It is more difficult to gauge accurately the impact of modern media on our values, attitudes, and expectations. Some people argue that the media merely reflect what is already going on, rather than actually making things happen. But there is little doubt that advertising uses both women and men as sex objects to sell products. In TV and movies, the "giving and receiving of the whole person" in marriage is often rejected as naïve. "Living together" is promoted as a wise option to marriage. Human fertility is viewed as an inconvenience to be avoided by using artificial contraception, rather than as a special gift of God to be shared with one's spouse.

Where do we find useful information that Christian couples can use in the development of a healthy Christian marriage?

A good starting point for reviewing our ideas about sexuality and sexual intercourse is the Bible. The Book of Genesis specifically describes the Lord God as creating human beings male and female and directing them to be fertile and multiply. The Creator offers this explanation: "It is not good for the man to be alone. I will make a suitable partner for him." To make sure we do not miss the point, the Lord God looks at the whole created universe — including humankind and sexuality — and says: "It is very good" (see Genesis 1:26–2:18).

Christianity promotes a vision of sexuality that (a) acknowledges the good and positive value of human sexuality, marital intimacy, and sexual intercourse; (b) affirms sexual intercourse as a special sign of permanent and total *marital* commitment; (c) teaches that there is a clear connection between the "lovemaking" and the "childbearing" dimensions of sexual intercourse; and (d) views fertility as a unique participation in the creative power of God.

Questions About Lovemaking, Fertility, and Parenthood

(Directions: These questions are for the sponsor couple. The engaged couple has slightly different questions. After each person has answered the questions on his or her page, the four people should share their responses.)

7. When and where and from whom did I first learn the biological facts about sexual intercourse and what were my feelings about learning this information? _____

8. When and where and from whom did I first learn the *meaning* of sexual intercourse and was this consistent with Christian teachings? _____

9. How successfully and appropriately do I incorporate physical expressions of affection into my relationships with my parents, other members of my family, male and female friends? Explain. _____

10. How well have I incorporated physical expressions of affection into my relationship with my spouse? _____

11. Which of these matters concerns me? (Check any that apply to you.)
    A. [ ] I worry that I have not been an adequate sex partner.
    B. [ ] I have often been afraid to initiate sexual intercourse.
    C. [ ] I am afraid of pregnancy.
    D. [ ] I am afraid of admitting any ignorance about sex.
    E. [ ] I sometimes worry about not pleasing my spouse.
    F. [ ] I find sex repulsive sometimes . . . often.
    G. [ ] I wonder if either of us has been exposed to AIDS.
    H. [ ] Sexual intercourse sometimes brings back bad memories.
    I. [ ] (other) _____

12. I would prefer that we celebrate sexual intercourse more often/less often/about as often as we have been (circle one).

13. What can we do to make sure that our experiences of lovemaking will be more satisfying for each of us? _____

14. What are the most important differences in our sexual responses that we have learned through our experience of lovemaking? _____

15. Do I view our fertility more as "gift" or as "problem to deal with?" Explain. _____

16. What are our plans for dealing with our gift of fertility as a couple? _____

(Note: In responding to the following questions about church teaching, answer according to the teaching of your own church. If your spouse is of a different denomination, his or her answers may be different from yours.)

17. What does my church teach about "responsible parenthood"? _____

18. What does my church teach about the use of family planning methods? _____

19. What do I understand about "natural family planning" and how does it differ from the "rhythm method"? _____

20. If we are not able to conceive children because one or both of us is infertile, how are we dealing with this? _____

Intimacy...An Essential Element of Christian Marriage

(Directions: The engaged couple and the sponsor couple should read the information on this page. They should discuss any ideas that need clarification before answering the questions that follow.)

Intimacy is a word that has many levels of meaning. For most people in our culture, intimacy suggests physical, even genital closeness. We hear, for example, that a friend is being intimate with her boyfriend; or we read in the newspaper about a sale on intimate apparel.

It is also important to reflect upon what we learned in our family of origin about intimacy. For many of us, intimate also meant "secret" and something "not to be discussed" with the children or even with one's spouse.

When we speak of intimacy in Christian marriage, however, we are not talking about something secretive. We are talking about a kind of mutual sharing that is physical, emotional, intellectual, and spiritual. Christian marriage is intimate when spouses share their thoughts, their feelings, their hopes, their dreams, their fears, their spirituality, their possessions, their responsibilities, their families, and also their physical selves with one another. When spouses share every part of their lives, they are truly

being intimate. It calls for a *total* sharing of one's person that respects and maintains the individual identity of both persons. In much the same way that Jesus and God are one, so Christian spouses become collaborative partners yet remain unique individuals (see John 17:21).

The "intimacy" of Christian marriage is difficult because it requires vulnerability. Vulnerability involves risk and even fear. The experience of Christians through the centuries is that our relationship with God encourages us to be intimate with one another. God's love for us makes us more alive rather than less alive; God's love for us makes us more free to be who we choose to be. Wise spouses know they can depend on the strength and power of God to help them risk deeper and deeper openness and intimacy with one another. They remember that "there is no fear in love, but perfect love drives out fear because fear has to do with punishment, and so one who fears is not yet perfect in love" (1 John 4:18).

Questions for Reflection and Dialogue

1. How did I experience intimacy in my family of origin? _____

_____

2. What does intimacy mean to me today? _____

_____

3. One aspect of intimacy involves the willingness to share my inner feelings with my spouse. Which feelings do I think I will find it difficult to share with my partner? (Check all that apply.)

A. [ ] bored   **F.** [ ] tender   **K.** [ ] joyful   **P.** [ ] sexually aroused
B. [ ] excited   **G.** [ ] angry   **L.** [ ] guilty   **Q.** [ ] distant
C. [ ] frustrated   **H.** [ ] afraid   **M.** [ ] anxious   **R.** [ ] isolated
D. [ ] jealous   **I.** [ ] ashamed   **N.** [ ] sad   **S.** [ ] close
E. [ ] embarrassed   **J.** [ ] lonely   **O.** [ ] silly   **T.** [ ] supported

4. What are my feelings about making a commitment to give of my "whole person" (thoughts, feelings, possessions, hopes, dreams, fears, and so forth) to my partner for a lifetime? _____

_____

5. What are several specific and practical things we can do to help us be more intimate as a Christian married couple? _____

_____

6. How does the intimacy of Christian marriage promote and encourage greater self-identity? _____

_____

(Directions: After answering the previous six questions, the couples should read the section below entitled "A Christian Vision of Sexuality, Marriage, and Parenthood" before answering questions 7-20. The sharing time with your partner and between the two couples will include questions 1-20.)

A Christian Vision of Sexuality, Marriage, and Parenthood

(Directions: The engaged couple and the sponsor couple should read the information on this page. They should discuss any ideas that need clarification before answering the questions that follow.)

Marriage is intended to be a way of life in which spouses strive to give themselves totally as a gift to one another at every level of their being. While sexuality is only one dimension of Christian marriage, it is necessary to pay particular attention to this topic because there are such contradictory views about the meaning of sexuality and sexual intercourse.

History is filled with examples of incorrect biological information leading to confused sociological and theological understandings of sexual intercourse and marital sexuality. Modern science has helped us see human sexuality and the processes of fertility much more accurately. Yet science can only tell us about the biology and physiology of sexuality and sexual intercourse. The *meaning* of sexuality and sexual intercourse comes from the fields of philosophy and religion. In today's society, however, there are many religions and philosophies teaching very different messages about the meaning of sexuality and sexual intercourse. This can cause confusion for engaged and married couples. Further confusion comes from inadequate sexual education and from the misinformation and hedonistic values espoused by TV, music, and advertising.

Most families, it seems, have done a poor job of sharing accurate information and Christian values and attitudes about sexuality and sexual intercourse. This is a primary reason that most "good Christians" do not really understand or live the Christian ideas and attitudes about sexuality and sexual intercourse. But, lest we be too hard on our parents, it is useful to remember that they, in turn, received poor information from their own parents.

It is more difficult to gauge accurately the impact of modern media on our values, attitudes, and expectations. Some people argue that the media merely reflect what is already going on, rather than actually making things happen. But there is little doubt that advertising uses both women and men as sex objects to sell products. In TV and movies, the "giving and receiving of the whole person" in marriage is often rejected as naïve. "Living together" is promoted as a wise option to marriage. Human fertility is viewed as an inconvenience to be avoided by using artificial contraception, rather than as a special gift of God to be shared with one's spouse.

Where do we find useful information that Christian couples can use in the development of a healthy Christian marriage?

A good starting point for reviewing our ideas about sexuality and sexual intercourse is the Bible. The Book of Genesis specifically describes the Lord God as creating human beings male and female and directing them to be fertile and multiply. The Creator offers this explanation: "It is not good for the man to be alone. I will make a suitable partner for him." To make sure we do not miss the point, the Lord God looks at the whole created universe — including humankind and sexuality — and says: "It is very good" (see Genesis 1:26–2:18).

Christianity promotes a vision of sexuality that (a) acknowledges the good and positive value of human sexuality, marital intimacy, and sexual intercourse; (b) affirms sexual intercourse as a special sign of permanent and total *marital* commitment; (c) teaches that there is a clear connection between the "lovemaking" and the "childbearing" dimensions of sexual intercourse; and (d) views fertility as a unique participation in the creative power of God.

Questions About Lovemaking, Fertility, and Parenthood

(Directions: These questions are for the sponsor couple. The engaged couple has slightly different questions. After each person has answered the questions on his or her page, the four people should share their responses.)

7. When and where and from whom did I first learn the biological facts about sexual intercourse and what were my feelings about learning this information? _____

8. When and where and from whom did I first learn the *meaning* of sexual intercourse and was this consistent with Christian teachings? _____

9. How successfully and appropriately do I incorporate physical expressions of affection into my relationships with my parents, other members of my family, male and female friends? Explain. _____

10. How well have I incorporated physical expressions of affection into my relationship with my spouse? _____

11. Which of these matters concerns me? (Check any that apply to you.)
    A. [ ] I worry that I have not been an adequate sex partner.
    B. [ ] I have often been afraid to initiate sexual intercourse.
    C. [ ] I am afraid of pregnancy.
    D. [ ] I am afraid of admitting any ignorance about sex.
    E. [ ] I sometimes worry about not pleasing my spouse.
    F. [ ] I find sex repulsive sometimes . . . often.
    G. [ ] I wonder if either of us has been exposed to AIDS.
    H. [ ] Sexual intercourse sometimes brings back bad memories.
    I. [ ] (other) _____

12. I would prefer that we celebrate sexual intercourse more often/less often/about as often as we have been (circle one).

13. What can we do to make sure that our experiences of lovemaking will be more satisfying for each of us? _____

14. What are the most important differences in our sexual responses that we have learned through our experience of lovemaking? _____

15. Do I view our fertility more as "gift" or as "problem to deal with?" Explain. _____

16. What are our plans for dealing with our gift of fertility as a couple? _____

(Note: In responding to the following questions about church teaching, answer according to the teaching of your own church. If your spouse is of a different denomination, his or her answers may be different from yours.)

17. What does my church teach about "responsible parenthood"? _____

18. What does my church teach about the use of family planning methods? _____

19. What do I understand about "natural family planning" and how does it differ from the "rhythm method"? _____

20. If we are not able to conceive children because one or both of us is infertile, how are we dealing with this? _____

EVENING **5**

A Covenant of Life and Love

Opening Prayer

A reading from Ecclesiastes 4:7-12.

Again I found this vanity under the sun: a solitary man with no companion; with neither son nor brother. Yet there is no end to all his toil, and riches do not satisfy his greed. "For whom do I toil and deprive myself of good things?" This also is vanity and a worthless task. Two are better than one: they get a good wage for their labor. If the one falls, the other will lift up his companion. Woe to the solitary man! For if he should fall, he has no one to lift him up. So also, if two sleep together, they keep each other warm. How can one alone keep warm? Where a lone man may be overcome, two together can resist. A three-ply cord is not easily broken.

The sponsor couple reads aloud the following prayer:

We thank you, dear Lord, for one another. We believe it is your Spirit that lighted our way to one another so that we could become a "two" that is "better than one." Individually and mutually, Lord, we commit ourselves to you. We ask you to be an inseparable part of our togetherness — a "three-ply cord" of husband, wife, and Christ — that is not easily broken. Help us to be faithful to you and to one another. Amen.

Closing Prayer

The engaged couple reads aloud the following prayer:

Lord God, as we come to the end of our evenings together as couples sharing with each other, we are at the beginning of an ever new and wonderful journey. We know more about where we have come from. We have remembered and shared the sorrows and the joys, the triumphs and defeats, of our past. We do not know what lies ahead for us. We know there will be pitfalls as well as pleasures. Our hours of happiness will be interrupted by times of despair. The path will sometimes be hard to find and difficult to travel. But we will be grateful, Lord, if you grant us the grace to continue our journey side-by-side.

May we discover in the midst of our most difficult hours that deep inner peace and joy of knowing that we are surrounded by your loving concern and that you will never depart from us.

We dedicate our lives to you, Lord, as our shepherd and our constant companion. Amen.

Christian Marriage — A Covenant of Unconditional Love

(Directions: The engaged couple and the sponsor couple should read the information on this page. They should discuss any ideas that need clarification before answering the questions that follow.)

A contract is a legal document which spells out the conditions of an agreement between two parties. If the conditions of the agreement are not met or the parties to the contract decide they are no longer satisfied with the contract, there are often provisions by which it can be terminated. Civil marriage is a contract that can be terminated by civil divorce.

A covenant is quite different from a contract. The relationship between God and the Chosen People is an example of a covenant. It calls for a relationship that is permanent and unconditional. Even if one party is unfaithful to this covenant or denies its existence, the covenant does not cease. God's covenant with us is unending.

Christian marriage has a religious dimension that may not be present in all civil marriages. Christian marriage looks to the wholeness (or "holy-ness") of each spouse. Holiness (or wholeness) is the result of the continuing physical, intellectual, emotional, and spiritual development of the person.

Christian marriage is a covenant, rather than a contract. Spouses are taught to commit themselves to one another in permanent and unconditional love. This commitment is intended to demonstrate to one's spouse and to other people a love that mirrors God's love for all people: "Husbands should love their wives . . . even as Christ does the Church" (Ephesians 5:28-29).

This covenant marriage (Christian marriage) involves a higher level of commitment than contract marriage (civil marriage). In Christian marriage the spouses freely commit to the lifelong responsibility of loving and serving one another. This assumes that the husband and wife are active Christians, committed to living their lives in accord with the Gospel. They intend their lives to be guided by the words and example of Christ who told his followers to "Love one another as I have loved you" (John 13:34). They also commit themselves to sharing their faith with their children, striving to "bring them up with the training and instruction of the Lord" (Ephesians 6:4).

Questions for Reflection and Dialogue

1. How was I taught to pray as a child, and what place did prayer have in my family when I was growing up?
_____
_____

2. What role does prayer play in my life at this time and how, why? What form does my prayer take?
_____
_____

3. How will we pray as a married couple and what effect will it have on our life together? _____
_____

4. How has our relationship affected my spiritual growth? _____
_____

5. What have my partner and I gained from discussing together our relationship with God? (If we have not experienced this kind of sharing, what prevents us?) _____
_____

6. Three religious practices that my partner has that support my own faith life are:
    A. _____
    B. _____
    C. _____

7. Two practices or behaviors in my partner that tend to hinder my own faith life are:
   A. _____
   B. _____

8. In what ways do my partner and I have a real understanding of and equal respect for each other's level of faith and religious practice? (This question applies even if you are of the same religious denomination.) _____

   _____

9. How can my partner and I be more supportive of each other's religious beliefs and practices? _____

   _____

10. Assuming that weekend worship and belonging to a church community are important elements of an active Christian faith life, how do we plan to celebrate weekend worship and participate in a church community? _____

    _____

(Note: In responding to the following questions about church teaching, answer according to the teaching of your own church. If your partner is of a different religion, his or her answer may be different from yours.)

11. What does my church teach about the meaning and importance of baptism of children and how do we plan to deal with this teaching in our marriage? _____

    _____

12. Are there any teachings of my church that I think will be difficult for us to follow in our marriage? _____

    _____

13. What is my attitude about the teaching authority of my church and what priority should this take in our marriage and family life? _____

    _____

14. Which teaching of my church do I find most challenging at the current time and how will this affect our marriage and family life? _____

    _____

15. The most important religious experience of my life has been _____

16. My spouse and I are choosing to celebrate our marriage within a particular Christian tradition because

    _____

    _____

Checklist for Comparing and Sharing Religious Values

Directions: For each item, list in the appropriate column:
  (1) your personal current values and feelings;
  (2) the values of your family of origin;
  (3) the values of your partner;
  (4) the values of your partner's family of origin.
You may have to guess about the values of your partner and his or her family of origin. Use these symbols:
  Very Important = +   Somewhat Important = O   Not Important = —

	1	2	3	4
A. Studying the Bible is	[ ]	[ ]	[ ]	[ ]
B. Learning more about the teachings of my church is	[ ]	[ ]	[ ]	[ ]
C. Registering as members of a parish is	[ ]	[ ]	[ ]	[ ]
D. Being actively involved in a parish is	[ ]	[ ]	[ ]	[ ]
E. Giving money to my church regularly is	[ ]	[ ]	[ ]	[ ]
F. Volunteering to help with service groups is	[ ]	[ ]	[ ]	[ ]
G. Having children is	[ ]	[ ]	[ ]	[ ]
H. Taking an active role in sharing my faith with our children is	[ ]	[ ]	[ ]	[ ]
I. Applying Christian values to my job is	[ ]	[ ]	[ ]	[ ]
J. Going to church each weekend is	[ ]	[ ]	[ ]	[ ]
K. Praying together as a couple is	[ ]	[ ]	[ ]	[ ]
L. Praying by myself is	[ ]	[ ]	[ ]	[ ]
M. Talking together about our relationship with God is	[ ]	[ ]	[ ]	[ ]
N. Setting aside time and money for my spiritual development is	[ ]	[ ]	[ ]	[ ]
O. Setting aside time and money to improve our love relationship is	[ ]	[ ]	[ ]	[ ]

Of all the above things, the three most important ones for us to agree upon are:

1. _____

2. _____

3. _____

Christian Marriage — A Covenant of Unconditional Love

(Directions: The engaged couple and the sponsor couple should read the information on this page. They should discuss any ideas that need clarification before answering the questions that follow.)

A contract is a legal document which spells out the conditions of an agreement between two parties. If the conditions of the agreement are not met or the parties to the contract decide they are no longer satisfied with the contract, there are often provisions by which it can be terminated. Civil marriage is a contract that can be terminated by civil divorce.

A covenant is quite different from a contract. The relationship between God and the Chosen People is an example of a covenant. It calls for a relationship that is permanent and unconditional. Even if one party is unfaithful to this covenant or denies its existence, the covenant does not cease. God's covenant with us is unending.

Christian marriage has a religious dimension that may not be present in all civil marriages. Christian marriage looks to the wholeness (or ''holy-ness'') of each spouse. Holiness (or wholeness) is the result of the continuing physical, intellectual, emotional, and spiritual development of the person.

Christian marriage is a covenant, rather than a contract. Spouses are taught to commit themselves to one another in permanent and unconditional love. This commitment is intended to demonstrate to one's spouse and to other people a love that mirrors God's love for all people: ''Husbands should love their wives . . . even as Christ does the Church'' (Ephesians 5:28-29).

This covenant marriage (Christian marriage) involves a higher level of commitment than contract marriage (civil marriage). In Christian marriage the spouses freely commit to the lifelong responsibility of loving and serving one another. This assumes that the husband and wife are active Christians, committed to living their lives in accord with the Gospel. They intend their lives to be guided by the words and example of Christ who told his followers to ''Love one another as I have loved you'' (John 13:34). They also commit themselves to sharing their faith with their children, striving to ''bring them up with the training and instruction of the Lord'' (Ephesians 6:4).

Questions for Reflection and Dialogue

1. How was I taught to pray as a child, and what place did prayer have in my family when I was growing up?

_____

_____

2. What role does prayer play in my life at this time and how, why? What form does my prayer take?

_____

_____

3. How will we pray as a married couple and what effect will it have on our life together? _____

_____

4. How has our relationship affected my spiritual growth? _____

_____

5. What have my partner and I gained from discussing together our relationship with God? (If we have not experienced this kind of sharing, what prevents us?) _____

_____

6. Three religious practices that my partner has that support my own faith life are:

A. _____

B. _____

C. _____

7. Two practices or behaviors in my partner that tend to hinder my own faith life are:

   A. _____

   B. _____

8. In what ways do my partner and I have a real understanding of and equal respect for each other's level of faith and religious practice? (This question applies even if you are of the same religious denomination.) _____

_____

9. How can my partner and I be more supportive of each other's religious beliefs and practices? _____

_____

10. Assuming that weekend worship and belonging to a church community are important elements of an active Christian faith life, how do we plan to celebrate weekend worship and participate in a church community? _____

_____

(Note: In responding to the following questions about church teaching, answer according to the teaching of your own church. If your partner is of a different religion, his or her answer may be different from yours.)

11. What does my church teach about the meaning and importance of baptism of children and how do we plan to deal with this teaching in our marriage? _____

_____

12. Are there any teachings of my church that I think will be difficult for us to follow in our marriage? _____

_____

13. What is my attitude about the teaching authority of my church and what priority should this take in our marriage and family life? _____

_____

14. Which teaching of my church do I find most challenging at the current time and how will this affect our marriage and family life? _____

_____

15. The most important religious experience of my life has been _____

16. My spouse and I are choosing to celebrate our marriage within a particular Christian tradition because

_____

_____

Checklist for Comparing and Sharing Religious Values

Directions: For each item, list in the appropriate column:
   (1) your personal current values and feelings;
   (2) the values of your family of origin;
   (3) the values of your partner;
   (4) the values of your partner's family of origin.
You may have to guess about the values of your partner and his or her family of origin. Use these symbols:
   Very Important = +   Somewhat Important = O   Not Important = —

	1	2	3	4
A. Studying the Bible is	[ ]	[ ]	[ ]	[ ]
B. Learning more about the teachings of my church is	[ ]	[ ]	[ ]	[ ]
C. Registering as members of a parish is	[ ]	[ ]	[ ]	[ ]
D. Being actively involved in a parish is	[ ]	[ ]	[ ]	[ ]
E. Giving money to my church regularly is	[ ]	[ ]	[ ]	[ ]
F. Volunteering to help with service groups is	[ ]	[ ]	[ ]	[ ]
G. Having children is	[ ]	[ ]	[ ]	[ ]
H. Taking an active role in sharing my faith with our children is	[ ]	[ ]	[ ]	[ ]
I. Applying Christian values to my job is	[ ]	[ ]	[ ]	[ ]
J. Going to church each weekend is	[ ]	[ ]	[ ]	[ ]
K. Praying together as a couple is	[ ]	[ ]	[ ]	[ ]
L. Praying by myself is	[ ]	[ ]	[ ]	[ ]
M. Talking together about our relationship with God is	[ ]	[ ]	[ ]	[ ]
N. Setting aside time and money for my spiritual development is	[ ]	[ ]	[ ]	[ ]
O. Setting aside time and money to improve our love relationship is	[ ]	[ ]	[ ]	[ ]

Of all the above things, the three most important ones for us to agree upon are:

1. _____

2. _____

3. _____

Christian Marriage — A Covenant of Unconditional Love

(Directions: The engaged couple and the sponsor couple should read the information on this page. They should discuss any ideas that need clarification before answering the questions that follow.)

A contract is a legal document which spells out the conditions of an agreement between two parties. If the conditions of the agreement are not met or the parties to the contract decide they are no longer satisfied with the contract, there are often provisions by which it can be terminated. Civil marriage is a contract that can be terminated by civil divorce.

A covenant is quite different from a contract. The relationship between God and the Chosen People is an example of a covenant. It calls for a relationship that is permanent and unconditional. Even if one party is unfaithful to this covenant or denies its existence, the covenant does not cease. God's covenant with us is unending.

Christian marriage has a religious dimension that may not be present in all civil marriages. Christian marriage looks to the wholeness (or "holy-ness") of each spouse. Holiness (or wholeness) is the result of the continuing physical, intellectual, emotional, and spiritual development of the person.

Christian marriage is a covenant, rather than a contract. Spouses are taught to commit themselves to one another in permanent and unconditional love. This commitment is intended to demonstrate to one's spouse and to other people a love that mirrors God's love for all people: "Husbands should love their wives . . . even as Christ does the Church" (Ephesians 5:28-29).

This covenant marriage (Christian marriage) involves a higher level of commitment than contract marriage (civil marriage). In Christian marriage the spouses freely commit to the lifelong responsibility of loving and serving one another. This assumes that the husband and wife are active Christians, committed to living their lives in accord with the Gospel. They intend their lives to be guided by the words and example of Christ who told his followers to "Love one another as I have loved you" (John 13:34). They also commit themselves to sharing their faith with their children, striving to "bring them up with the training and instruction of the Lord" (Ephesians 6:4).

Questions for Reflection and Dialogue

1. How was I taught to pray as a child, and what place did prayer have in my family when I was growing up?

2. What role does prayer play in my life at this time and how, why? What form does my prayer take?

3. How will we pray as a married couple and what effect will it have on our life together?

4. How has our relationship affected my spiritual growth?

5. What have my partner and I gained from discussing together our relationship with God? (If we have not experienced this kind of sharing, what prevents us?)

6. Three religious practices that my partner has that support my own faith life are:

   A.

   B.

   C.

7. Two practices or behaviors in my partner that tend to hinder my own faith life are:
   A. _____
   B. _____

8. In what ways do my partner and I have a real understanding of and equal respect for each other's level of faith and religious practice? (This question applies even if you are of the same religious denomination.) _____

9. How can my partner and I be more supportive of each other's religious beliefs and practices? _____

10. Assuming that weekend worship and belonging to a church community are important elements of an active Christian faith life, how do we plan to celebrate weekend worship and participate in a church community? _____

(Note: In responding to the following questions about church teaching, answer according to the teaching of your own church. If your partner is of a different religion, his or her answer may be different from yours.)

11. What does my church teach about the meaning and importance of baptism of children and how do we plan to deal with this teaching in our marriage? _____

12. Are there any teachings of my church that I think will be difficult for us to follow in our marriage? _____

13. What is my attitude about the teaching authority of my church and what priority should this take in our marriage and family life? _____

14. Which teaching of my church do I find most challenging at the current time and how will this affect our marriage and family life? _____

15. The most important religious experience of my life has been _____

16. My spouse and I are choosing to celebrate our marriage within a particular Christian tradition because _____

Checklist for Comparing and Sharing Religious Values

Directions: For each item, list in the appropriate column:
  (1) your personal current values and feelings;
  (2) the values of your family of origin;
  (3) the values of your partner;
  (4) the values of your partner's family of origin.
You may have to guess about the values of your partner and his or her family of origin. Use these symbols:
  Very Important = +   **Somewhat Important = O**   **Not Important = —**

	1	2	3	4
A. Studying the Bible is	[ ]	[ ]	[ ]	[ ]
B. Learning more about the teachings of my church is	[ ]	[ ]	[ ]	[ ]
C. Registering as members of a parish is	[ ]	[ ]	[ ]	[ ]
D. Being actively involved in a parish is	[ ]	[ ]	[ ]	[ ]
E. Giving money to my church regularly is	[ ]	[ ]	[ ]	[ ]
F. Volunteering to help with service groups is	[ ]	[ ]	[ ]	[ ]
G. Having children is	[ ]	[ ]	[ ]	[ ]
H. Taking an active role in sharing my faith with our children is	[ ]	[ ]	[ ]	[ ]
I. Applying Christian values to my job is	[ ]	[ ]	[ ]	[ ]
J. Going to church each weekend is	[ ]	[ ]	[ ]	[ ]
K. Praying together as a couple is	[ ]	[ ]	[ ]	[ ]
L. Praying by myself is	[ ]	[ ]	[ ]	[ ]
M. Talking together about our relationship with God is	[ ]	[ ]	[ ]	[ ]
N. Setting aside time and money for my spiritual development is	[ ]	[ ]	[ ]	[ ]
O. Setting aside time and money to improve our love relationship is	[ ]	[ ]	[ ]	[ ]

Of all the above things, the three most important ones for us to agree upon are:

1. _____

2. _____

3. _____

Christian Marriage — A Covenant of Unconditional Love

(Directions: The engaged couple and the sponsor couple should read the information on this page. They should discuss any ideas that need clarification before answering the questions that follow.)

A contract is a legal document which spells out the conditions of an agreement between two parties. If the conditions of the agreement are not met or the parties to the contract decide they are no longer satisfied with the contract, there are often provisions by which it can be terminated. Civil marriage is a contract that can be terminated by civil divorce.

A covenant is quite different from a contract. The relationship between God and the Chosen People is an example of a covenant. It calls for a relationship that is permanent and unconditional. Even if one party is unfaithful to this covenant or denies its existence, the covenant does not cease. God's covenant with us is unending.

Christian marriage has a religious dimension that may not be present in all civil marriages. Christian marriage looks to the wholeness (or "holy-ness") of each spouse. Holiness (or wholeness) is the result of the continuing physical, intellectual, emotional, and spiritual development of the person.

Christian marriage is a covenant, rather than a contract. Spouses are taught to commit themselves to one another in permanent and unconditional love. This commitment is intended to demonstrate to one's spouse and to other people a love that mirrors God's love for all people: "Husbands should love their wives . . . even as Christ does the Church" (Ephesians 5:28-29).

This covenant marriage (Christian marriage) involves a higher level of commitment than contract marriage (civil marriage). In Christian marriage the spouses freely commit to the lifelong responsibility of loving and serving one another. This assumes that the husband and wife are active Christians, committed to living their lives in accord with the Gospel. They intend their lives to be guided by the words and example of Christ who told his followers to "Love one another as I have loved you" (John 13:34). They also commit themselves to sharing their faith with their children, striving to "bring them up with the training and instruction of the Lord" (Ephesians 6:4).

Questions for Reflection and Dialogue

1. How was I taught to pray as a child, and what place did prayer have in my family when I was growing up?

   _____

2. What role does prayer play in my life at this time and how, why? What form does my prayer take?

   _____

3. How will we pray as a married couple and what effect will it have on our life together? _____

   _____

4. How has our relationship affected my spiritual growth? _____

   _____

5. What have my partner and I gained from discussing together our relationship with God? (If we have not experienced this kind of sharing, what prevents us?) _____

   _____

6. Three religious practices that my partner has that support my own faith life are:

   A. _____

   B. _____

   C. _____

7. Two practices or behaviors in my partner that tend to hinder my own faith life are:
   A. _____
   B. _____

8. In what ways do my partner and I have a real understanding of and equal respect for each other's level of faith and religious practice? (This question applies even if you are of the same religious denomination.) _____

   _____

9. How can my partner and I be more supportive of each other's religious beliefs and practices? _____

   _____

10. Assuming that weekend worship and belonging to a church community are important elements of an active Christian faith life, how do we plan to celebrate weekend worship and participate in a church community? _____

    _____

(Note: In responding to the following questions about church teaching, answer according to the teaching of your own church. If your partner is of a different religion, his or her answer may be different from yours.)

11. What does my church teach about the meaning and importance of baptism of children and how do we plan to deal with this teaching in our marriage? _____

    _____

12. Are there any teachings of my church that I think will be difficult for us to follow in our marriage? _____

    _____

13. What is my attitude about the teaching authority of my church and what priority should this take in our marriage and family life? _____

    _____

14. Which teaching of my church do I find most challenging at the current time and how will this affect our marriage and family life? _____

    _____

15. The most important religious experience of my life has been _____

16. My spouse and I are choosing to celebrate our marriage within a particular Christian tradition because

    _____

    _____

Checklist for Comparing and Sharing Religious Values

Directions: For each item, list in the appropriate column:
  (1) your personal current values and feelings;
  (2) the values of your family of origin;
  (3) the values of your partner;
  (4) the values of your partner's family of origin.
You may have to guess about the values of your partner and his or her family of origin. Use these symbols:
  Very Important = +   Somewhat Important = O   Not Important = —

	1	2	3	4
A. Studying the Bible is	[ ]	[ ]	[ ]	[ ]
B. Learning more about the teachings of my church is	[ ]	[ ]	[ ]	[ ]
C. Registering as members of a parish is	[ ]	[ ]	[ ]	[ ]
D. Being actively involved in a parish is	[ ]	[ ]	[ ]	[ ]
E. Giving money to my church regularly is	[ ]	[ ]	[ ]	[ ]
F. Volunteering to help with service groups is	[ ]	[ ]	[ ]	[ ]
G. Having children is	[ ]	[ ]	[ ]	[ ]
H. Taking an active role in sharing my faith with our children is	[ ]	[ ]	[ ]	[ ]
I. Applying Christian values to my job is	[ ]	[ ]	[ ]	[ ]
J. Going to church each weekend is	[ ]	[ ]	[ ]	[ ]
K. Praying together as a couple is	[ ]	[ ]	[ ]	[ ]
L. Praying by myself is	[ ]	[ ]	[ ]	[ ]
M. Talking together about our relationship with God is	[ ]	[ ]	[ ]	[ ]
N. Setting aside time and money for my spiritual development is	[ ]	[ ]	[ ]	[ ]
O. Setting aside time and money to improve our love relationship is	[ ]	[ ]	[ ]	[ ]

Of all the above things, the three most important ones for us to agree upon are:

1. _____

2. _____

3. _____

Preparing the Marriage Ceremony

Again, [amen,] I say to you, if two of you agree on earth about anything for which they are to pray, it shall be granted to them by my heavenly Father. For where two or three are gathered together in my name, there am I in the midst of them.

Matthew 18:19-20

Your marriage ceremony is one of the most important events in your life. The priest and the congregation are the witnesses of your vows to each other and to the Lord. The actual ministers of the sacrament of Matrimony, however, are you and your partner. For this reason, you are invited to plan this special liturgy yourselves.

In the beginning of Christianity there was no special Christian marriage ritual. People married according to the custom of their family or tribe and then asked the bishop for a blessing. Only in the Middle Ages did the marriage ceremony itself begin to take place in the Church.

Except for the Scripture readings and the statement of the vows, most of the traditions and customs associated with the weddings of Christians are actually ancient Jewish, Roman, or Greek family customs. The "giving away" of the bride, the exchange of rings, the tossing of rice, the use of wine, the sharing of a cake, and the carrying of the bride over the threshold (The groom had to sneak her past the household gods who would be expected to treat her as an alien and do her harm.) are all pagan traditions from ancient Rome.

Since the 1960s, it has become the custom in most Christian churches for couples to plan their wedding liturgy in a manner that is suitable to Christian ideas and traditions while also reflecting the faith life and personalities of the couple. It is hoped that couples today have the education to see that many of the pagan traditions of the past are inappropriate to Christian marriage. For example, the "giving away of the bride" by her father meant that the father *owned* his daughter and was giving her to a new owner; the fact that only the bride was given a ring meant that only she was "bound" to fidelity in the marriage.

Today we see couples using newly developed rituals that are more suited to a Christian understanding of marriage. The meeting of both families often replaces the giving away of the bride by her father. The use of two rings shows that both are equally committed to permanent and faithful love. The lighting of a Unity Candle indicates the union of the two becoming one.

During the weeks and months of preparation for your wedding, you have had the opportunity to reflect on and deepen your love for each other. You have also had the time to discuss how your love is a special gift from God and a sign of God's own permanent and unconditional love. In planning your wedding liturgy you will have an opportunity to put into words and actions what your marriage commitment means to you.

Get in touch with a priest in your parish, who will tell you what you need to know about planning your wedding ceremony and give you the necessary materials.

Family Life Products From Liguori Publications

PRAYERS FOR MARRIED COUPLES
by Renee Bartkowski

Contains more than 75 brief prayers that express the hopes, concerns, and dreams of today's married couple. With this book as a guide, two people can share prayers, reflecting a rainbow of circumstances. **$4.95**

SHARING THE FAITH WITH YOUR CHILD
(From Birth to Age Six)
A Handbook for Catholic Parents
by Phyllis Chandler and Joan Burney

Invaluable book for parents of a small child. Discusses rearing children in a Christian family, parents as models, siblings, and more. **$3.95**

HANDBOOK FOR TODAY'S CATHOLIC FAMILY
A Redemptorist Pastoral Publication

Basic ideas in Catholic theology for today's family, questions for reflection and dialogue, ideas for family prayer. **$4.95**

HOW TO SURVIVE BEING MARRIED TO A CATHOLIC
A Redemptorist Pastoral Publication

Using a lively cartoon format, along with pages of text, this book gives clear and honest answers to these and many other questions often asked by non-Catholic partners in interfaith marriages. If offers down-to-earth information about what Catholics believe and what difference it makes in their lives. **$6.95**

FAMILY PLANNING
A Guide for Exploring the Issues
by Charles and Elizabeth Balsam

This third edition offers a concise overview of family planning methods, their effectiveness, their side effects, and health risks. It also explains Church teaching on the subject, showing why Natural Family Planning (NFP) fulfills the holistic personal moral vision upheld by Christian tradition. **$1.95**

SAINTLY CELEBRATIONS AND HOLY HOLIDAYS
Bernadette McCarver Snyder

Even in today's hurried, hectic world, no matter how busy we are, we can create family celebrations that are sure to be stored in every member's memory for years to come.

Inside are may pick-and-choose ways to put "red letter days" into every month of the year. Every idea is practical and possible—and has been family tested for fun and excitement.

Celebrations include: • Monthly Saints' Days • Un-Birthdays • A Winter Picnic • An Ash Wednesday Alleluia • Mother's Day Mud Pies and Dirt Cakes • Prayer Pretzels • A "Holy Halo" Feast of the Archangels • And many more! **$9.95**

Order from your local bookstore or write
Liguori Publications
Box 060, Liguori, MO 63057-9999
Please add 15% to the total for shipping and handling
($3.50 minimum, $15 maximum). For faster service on orders
over $20, call toll-free 1-800-325-9521, Dept. 060.
Please have your credit card ready.